Darrin & Me

Love has no boundaries.

Darrin King and Meredith Collins

Darrin & Me

Love has no boundaries.

The Sandusky and Fairview Heights neighborhoods in Lynchburg, Virginia were only 11 miles apart, but they may as well have been on different planets in 1987 for all they had in common. The dissimilarities in the lifestyles of those living in the two neighborhoods was noticeable. It wasn't just a disparity in income levels that created the differences. It was also the culture, a way of life that that differed not simply due to money, skin color, or opportunities. In Fairview Heights, life was simply harder. Fortunately, neighborhoods are made up of individuals and individuals can choose to understand differences and look past them to embrace the things they do have in common, like hopes and dreams and aspirations – and even pizza.

The hand of God was truly at work when the 27 year old Meredith White of Sandusky Drive and 8 year old Darrin King of Gilmore Circle came into each other's orbit. A world of differences were irrelevant or just didn't matter. Over time they didn't allow such things as age, gender, race, income or anything else to define their relationship. Those things were stripped away to breathe life into more important matters. They lived in the moments they were given. Originally brought together by the Big Brothers and Big Sisters organization, their friendship far outgrew that program and continues to blossom today. This is a story of an unpredictable and indescribable bond that was forged by two individuals who were indifferent to their differences and grew to love one another with no boundaries.

"As the leader of a local Big Brothers Big Sisters organization for almost two decades, I certainly understand the impact that mentoring can have. But it is always the mentee that we believe receives all the benefits of a mentoring relationship. What we don't talk about as often is the impact that mentoring can have on the mentor themselves. *Darrin & Me* shines a light on an amazing relationship from both perspectives and illustrates how love can soothe the hurt of a painful past and motivate one to live a better life."

Ash Gorman
Executive Director,
Big Brothers Big Sisters of Central Virginia

"*Darrin and Me* is a wonderful story of what happens when you only want the very best for those you care about. The authors, Meredith Collins and Darrin King, came together through the Big Brothers and Big Sisters organization. In many ways, they were an unlikely match. Yet their life adventures and connections teach us that real love can help us overcome the most trying of circumstances. And that real love makes our life's milestones and celebrations more wonderful and joyful."

Rob Brown
Author, *Truest Fan: Live, Love & Lead with Purpose & Impact*

"Every once in a while we run into someone who is unique. They seem to be marching to a different drummer than most of society and are pleased with their responsive approach to life.. This person doesn't seem to be enamored by the labels that are used to identify the various factors that comprise our communities, such as male/female, old/young, rich/poor, black/white, and so on. This person seems to recognize when someone is hurting and avails themselves with what they can offer. This person does not look for rewards or recognition for the service they provide, in fact they consider it as the purpose of life. They seem to be very comfortable in the life they live and invite others to join them. Such a person is Meredith Collins."

Bill Forloine, Friend and Mentor

Darrin & Me

Love has no boundaries.

www. darrinandme.com

For orders or inquiries, please use the form on the website.

Contributors and Editors:
Linda Landreth Phelps, Narielle Living,
Joe Collins and Ginger White

ISBN: 978-0-578-36194-9

First Edition: January 2022

To the reader:

The content provided in Darrin & Me is true. However, due to the sensitive nature of some of the material presented in this book, some of the names have been changed.

This book is dedicated to Patricia King,
who never got to see what a good man her son became.

Chapter 1
Big and Little

As I walked up the well worn sidewalk to my first meeting with eight-year-old Darrin King, I somehow knew that once I entered the home it led to my life would change irrevocably. In 1987, Darrin was small and handsome with penetrating, inquisitive eyes as he fidgeted next to his mom on the couch of their sparsely decorated living room. Proudly displayed family photos showcased three children, with the child on the left being Darrin. A caseworker for Big Brothers and Big Sisters (BBBS) and I were there to discuss the possibility of me becoming Darrin's Big Sister. I was a little nervous, but eager too since all of the paperwork was now finished and my journey as a volunteer was about to begin.

BBBS, a national organization with chapters throughout the United States, makes meaningful, monitored matches between adult volunteers and youngsters with an aim to develop positive relationships that have a direct and lasting effect on the lives of young people. I volunteered in my hometown of Lynchburg where I grew up.

While BBBS sets up the matches, it's up to the Bigs and Littles to make it work and to make it meaningful. All volunteers must agree to spend a minimum of three hours a week with their child. Sometimes volunteers discover they can't make this kind of commitment. Maybe they just can't relate to their Little, or the relationship doesn't grow, or their personal lives change; sometimes, life just gets in the way. When that happens, the child may get hurt and the adult often feels guilty, and it can turn out to be negative for both parties. For reasons that were somewhat altruistic and very personal, I definitely did not want that to happen with my Little Brother. I was on a mission to prove something to myself and the world, and I was ready. I looked at Darrin as he sat on the sofa with his mother, his hands clasped in his lap, his expectant eyes alert to what was going on in the room. He knew change was in the air, but what it was, he wasn't sure. Neither was I.

"Want to get a milkshake from Burger King?" I asked. His big brown eyes lit up, and he smiled.

"Yes," Darrin replied. He glanced at his mom for permission and she reassured him with a nod. And so it began.

Weeks earlier, I had applied to become a volunteer for BBBS. That meant a thorough background check and intensive interview. I was less of an unknown quantity than most volunteers would have been because I had served on their board, a position I resigned so that I could volunteer directly with a child rather than sit in meetings talking about them. For the first time the local organization was willing to match a female Big Sister with a Little Brother since there was a chronic shortage of male volunteers. Matching me, a 27-year-old white woman, with Darrin, an eight-year-old black boy, was progressive, but it was also an experiment to see if young boys would benefit from mentoring by a woman instead of a man.

Darrin, his sister, Bernice and brother, Will, with their Mom.

The first file folder the caseworker had shared with me was for a boy who had emotional problems that I wasn't sure I could handle. Could I cope with a 12-year- old wetting his pants? Were his emotional problems rooted in the circumstances of his home life? With my history, I was anxious not to get in over my head.

The next file was labeled "Darrin Anthony King." He was living in Lynchburg's Fairview Heights with his mom, brother and sister. It was a single parent household as his father had died when Darrin was quite young. The file photo of Darrin revealed a sweet-looking kid with alert eyes and neatly trimmed hair. I wondered what his mom would think of this match. No doubt she had been waiting a long time for a man to come into Darrin's life but it had never happened. There was such a shortage of male volunteers that many boys were stuck forever on a waiting list, growing up without ever having a Big Brother to serve as an adult mentor and friend. Thirty-five years later as I write this, it is still, sadly, a challenge for the organization.

After we met, Darrin's mother, Patricia, asked questions of the caseworker while I took Darrin up the street to a Burger King. We had created this little diversion to give Patricia enough time to decide if she would consider me to be the right fit for her son. I ordered milkshakes for us and we sat at one of the booths to enjoy them.

Darrin drank his milkshake slowly. His short legs didn't reach the floor, and he nervously swung them a bit. Our conversation was light, easy things about school and his friends.

"What grade are you in?" I asked.

"Fifth," he said.

"Do you like it?

"It's okay," he replied.

Simple questions didn't really elicit amazing answers, but we began to build a rapport between us. He wasn't exactly shy, just reserved and sizing up the situation, trying to figure out how he felt about me. On my part, I liked Darrin immediately, but I still had some doubts about myself in this situation. Would I be a good mentor? Would I be able to meet the minimum required three hours a week with him? With me being a woman, would we be able to connect emotionally? I put these negative thoughts aside and focused on how I genuinely liked kids and knew how crucial the right kind of adults are in a young person's life. In the time it takes to drink a milkshake, I already knew that if Darrin would have me as his Big Sister, I wanted him as my Little Brother.

We slurped our drinks down to the last noisy drops, tossed the cups in the trash, and drove back down the hill to his house. Once we went inside, the caseworker asked him if he would like for me to be his Big Sister. He looked at his mom and smiled. I was happy and a little nervous, but confident that being female would be an obstacle only if I let it be. After all, hadn't I grown up as a tomboy? As a kid, I could climb trees and throw a football with the guys as well as or better than anyone in my neighborhood. I played basketball in high school and went on to attend the University of North Carolina on a basketball scholarship.

That was one sport I knew I could teach Darrin, should he have the interest. Yeah, this was going to be a great experience for us both. It was also going to be a meaningful way for me to grow in ways I couldn't imagine.

Since Darrin was an athletic kid, I figured he would know who Michael Jordan was, despite his young age. I tried to yank his chain a little with a story I have told frequently, one that is a joke, of course.

"Darrin, did you know Michael Jordan played basketball at UNC while I was there on the women's team?" I said.

"No," he replied.

"He did. That's true," I said.

"Really?"

"Yep, and you know what? I taught him everything he knows about basketball, especially those dunks where he flies through the air."

Darrin laughed. He might have been young, but he wasn't stupid. I knew we were going to have fun together.

I knew my success in this volunteer role would be closely tied to a personal motivation. I wanted to prove to myself that an adult could care about a young person in a healthy way and become an exceptional mentor who could make a positive difference in that young person's life. I wanted that mentor to be me, and I wanted to be exceptional. My feelings about becoming a good mentor had everything to do with events that impacted my young life in a profoundly negative way. With Darrin, I was hoping for a do-over, one with a dramatically different outcome than my own.

Darrin with my cardboard cutout of Michael Jordan.

***

My mom started to realize that me and my brother, Willie, needed something positive to do with all the time we had on our hands while she was at work. So she got us involved in Pee Wee football. I played for about a year, and I found out that I really loved the sport, but it wasn't enough to keep me or Willie busy. So, that's when Mom thought the Big Brother and Big Sister program could contribute to us. My mom never told me or Willie that we were on the Big Brother waiting list so when she told me a guy named Don from the Big Brother program wanted to meet me and Willie, I was shocked. Don turned out to be pretty cool. He used to come get my brother and me about every other week and take us to the park or his house. He only lasted a few months, though. He had to move, so that was the end of that.

My next Big Brother turned out to be my Big Sister, Meredith. It took me about a year to get matched up with her. My mom told me that it was going to be a woman instead of a man about a week before I met her. I guess Mom wanted to know how I felt about the whole thing. I told her I felt all right about everything, but I really didn't. I thought that she was just a girl and couldn't possibly like the things I like. Everything I needed to know I got from my mom, so what could she teach me?

The day finally came for me to meet Meredith, and I was nervous as hell. I remember when she first pulled up to the house, me and Willie were looking out the window and I thought the caseworker who was with Meredith, was Meredith. I ran through the house yelling, "She's pretty!" and Willie said, "That's our caseworker, dummy." Defensively, I told him that Meredith was pretty too, and ran into the living room to finally meet her.

When I met Meredith, that was a brand new experience just being with a lady, a female, but it wasn't like I was nervous or scared or anything, I was like, I'm ready. And she was nice. I mean, when we first went out and we talked, that conversation put me at ease. I can't remember what she said, but I was never nervous or anxious. I looked forward to meeting her and later was comfortable calling her to see if we could do something that week. It started off like that.

*Darrin wearing a Carolina sweatshirt,
which I got him, of course.
He is still a UNC fan today.*

Chapter 2
Beginnings

Until I turned 13, my early childhood was pretty normal. My dad, Al White, was a Virginia Tech graduate. He worked as an electrical engineer, first for Lynchburg Foundry, and later for CB Fleet. My mother, June Mason White, stayed at home with my brother and sister and I when we were young, then worked as a registered nurse at Virginia Baptist Hospital. David was four years older with friends his own age, and not inclined to hang out with a little sister who had different interests. My older sister, Ginger, was closer to me. She was slender, with olive skin and a pretty face, a good swimmer who competed in swim meets and earned quite a few medals. She attracted the attention of many boys when she was a teenager. I did not. I wanted to be outdoors all the time and was somewhat of a loner.

I wasn't just an introvert, however. I didn't understand, and neither did my parents, that I was dealing with mental health issues, even as a child. Anxiety, even when there was no apparent reason for it, was my constant companion, and I often lived inside my own head. Once, when I was eight or nine, I sat in my backyard under a tree, plucking individual hairs from my head and creating a bald spot the size of a half dollar. I also yanked out all of my eyelashes. As an adult, I learned that this condition is called trichotillomania, an impulse control disorder, and apparently a way to self-soothe and cope with stress. But in 1968 my mom had no name for it, and she was simply horrified. She took me to see a pediatrician. Following his advice, my mom purchased a little stuffed gray mouse with a pink tail and told me to pet it anytime I thought I might pull my hair. I hated that mouse.

I was chronically depressed then, but skilled at hiding it. I was very competent at school, getting A's and B's in every grade since I started attending school. Other kids liked me, but I did not like myself. I felt different, and I did not know how to change it. My mom was a pretty good nurturer with all of her children. My dad was less demonstrative and more of a disciplinarian. They also fought a lot, never physically, typically just loud screaming and crying. I couldn't stand to hear them and would often escape out the back door and sit on the curb on the street behind us. I felt inadequate, as though I should find a way to fix all of that. I wasn't even sure if my parents loved each other. From time to time there were glimpses of a loving marriage, but mostly I felt only tension inside our home. As problematic as their marriage was, not all of their parenting was bad.

In fact, even then I felt lucky to have parents as capable as them, and I was aware many kids were not so lucky.

My folks did a good job teaching us values and helping us to understand that hard work, and good work, was to be strived for. They were attentive and involved in our lives and made sure we had good meals, nice clothes to wear to school, and a good life to look forward to. After the hair-pulling episodes, my mom understood that I had some mental health issues going on and enrolled me in art classes as therapy. I had always liked to draw and that seemed to be a good outlet for me. Better than that damn mouse.

Even so, I seemed to need more than what I got at home. I always felt guilty, as if somehow my difference was my fault. No one else in our family had these problems. My anxiety led to a huge sense of being lost. Sometimes I would go to the street behind our house just to be by myself. But I didn't stay alone. Sitting on the curb there led me to meet new friends who lived on that block. Most of them were around my age, so we played basketball and spent time doing what kids do.

Occasionally, my Mom would march down to the back street, standing in a neighbor's yard, looking for me. She would spot me across the street with the other kids and raise her voice at me.

"Meredith, I told you to finish your ironing before you came down here," she scolded me.

"I did, Mom," I said.

"No, you didn't finish. You need to come home right now," she demanded.

"Okay, Mom," I replied reluctantly, and left my friends to trudge home. Typically, it was only one garment I'd left un-ironed, not a wrinkled pile. I couldn't make any sense of why she was so upset over small things like one piece of clothing. She also tended to have emotional extremes that I couldn't predict or explain.

That back street became my haven, somewhere I could hang out without worrying about any tension at home or even what was wrong with me. I made one new friend there who helped me feel better about myself than I ever had before, and also, eventually, the absolute worst. That person changed my life forever.

Doug and Betty Adams were new to the Sandusky neighborhood. They were in their mid-forties and had three children, Ron, who was an adult, and Teresa and Reggie, both close in age to me. To my thirteen-year-old mind, this family represented everything my family had never been, nor could be. They not only liked me, they also seemed to look forward to times when I came around. I was drawn almost immediately to Doug, the dad, and thrived on the attention he and his family gave me. Doug was particularly attentive, and I admired him and put him on a pedestal. His approval, attention, laughter and focus fed my wounded inner self like nothing else ever had.

In the Adams's home, I felt like a bright spot in their lives. I joked and told stories, and every time I made them laugh, I felt a warm swell of satisfaction. I craved Doug and his reactions. It could have been a vulnerable time in his life then, when he had tired of his drab marriage, or his dull job. As I only learned much later, it must also have been because he, too, was not well emotionally and mentally that Doug became as preoccupied with me as I was with him. I would punch him playfully or mess with him jokingly, whatever it took to get a response from him. I would sit for countless hours talking to Doug and making jokes. Sometimes other family members would be there, too, but I was never chastised for anything I said. I felt encouraged to express every thought freely, no matter how inappropriate or crude. It seemed I could do no wrong within those walls, a vast contrast with my life at home, where I felt like my father rarely listened to me.

My new enthusiasm for the Adams family soon became apparent to my parents. I talked about Doug, particularly, quite often at the dinner table. The more enthusiasm I expressed for that family, the more resentment my parents showed and the more negative their comments became. Looking back, I know the things I said must have hurt them deeply, especially since they could tell I seemed happier. I know they were concerned, but I don't think they were concerned about the right things. Were they really that naïve? My relationship with Doug was evolving into a train wreck, and with most of my teen years ahead of me, surely my parents should have wondered where all of this was heading. In the early 1970s, however, most people weren't as alert to those red flags as they are today.

The more my parents expressed their displeasure, the more I retreated to the Adams home. After all, I thought and felt that, for the first time in my life, I was feeling loved, appreciated, and important. At their house, my opinion was not only valued, it was sought after and even respected. This contrast began to breed anger and resentment toward my parents, and I alienated myself from them even more. I decided if they didn't want to hear about my joys in life, I wouldn't share them with them. And so I didn't. From that time on, I rarely spoke of the Adams and my life on the back street. That distancing from my parents became the turning point on the course I would take, the precise spot where the train began to derail.

The more I began to bask in Doug's approval and acceptance, the more my own father suffered in comparison. Feelings of irritation when I was around Dad quickly ballooned into feelings of contempt. I am ashamed, as I reflect on how much hatred I felt; I was intolerant, cold and unreceptive to him. I hated being around him, and I chose not to be when I could. If I was in his company, I found it difficult to hide my bubbling anger and resentment. I can't imagine how much that must have hurt him, especially since he had no clue why I'd turned on him. Doug's example of how I thought a father should be made me resent my dad for all the things that he had withheld. The changed dynamics in my family illustrated that I had closed the door on the only people who really loved me and had chosen instead some of the most warped people I have ever known. I went into that situation innocently, with childlike belief, trust and love. For many years I remained that emotionally needy, misled child. It was this which made what followed so devastating.

The first thing I noticed, which in a healthier child might have been a big red flag or at least a reason to tell Mom about it, is that Doug tried to create special moments with me. He would go to work around five a.m., and he told me if I would look out my bedroom window he would wave at me. My bedroom was on the front side of our house, and my bed was positioned directly beside the window. He was testing me, putting his toe in the water so to speak, but I had no idea. I woke up and watched for him, and I could hear the hum of his Volkswagen as it went down the street and approached our house. He slowed down and waved at me. This became a regular occurrence and our little secret.

The transition to emotional and sexual abuse occurred over time, and its foundation was rooted in my absolute trust and desire for Doug's acceptance and approval. My whole life began to be centered on being in his company. When I was with him, I felt complete. When we were apart, I became anxious and unsettled. I associated being with Doug with feeling good, and naively labeled these feelings as love. I became addicted to the "up" feelings I could get in his presence, and the "down" feelings I had when I was apart from him were unbearable. Was he aware of my low self-esteem and need for him, his power over me? Anybody who cared to notice could see how I lit up in his company. It was this control, the 45-year-old adult over the 13-year-old child, that he used to satisfy his own wants and needs.

Although I thought of Doug in terms of love, I know as an adult that what happened had nothing to do with love at all. As the author, M. Scott Peck, defines it, "Love is the will to extend one's self for the purpose of nurturing one's own or another's spiritual growth." It is not dependency, control, selfishness, relief from anxiety, excitement or any other self-serving feeling. It implies giving, not taking. What Doug did with me took what little self I had.

I remember clearly the first time Doug hugged me, and how it felt. I was 15 years old and my family was vacationing at Myrtle Beach, South Carolina, and his family happened to be there at the same time. My parents thought it would be fun for me to spend the day with Doug's kids, so I went to their hotel and spent the day on the beach with them. While we were out in the ocean, far away from his own family, who couldn't swim as well as I could, Doug pulled me close and hugged me in a full-body intimacy that sparked fireworks in my teenaged brain. The cool ocean waters were no match for the heat that hug ignited. "Grooming" wasn't a word I understood then, but he did.

When Doug first began touching me in ways that were not "fatherly", he would stroke my legs, or play with my hair. I knew there was more in his touch than fatherly approval. At 15, I felt uneasy around boys my own age. Emotionally stunted, I didn't seek out my peers for their friendships or learn who I was through trial and error. I had school friends then, but I didn't pursue after-school friendships. I clung even closer to the seemingly safe, comfortable environment of the Adams' home.

Doug's touches had awakened natural curiosity and enthusiasm for newly discovered sensations. Along with the good feelings of sexual awareness and stimulation came a flood of negative emotions associated with these things originating in an adult, married man who was thirty years older. I couldn't help being aware that what we were doing was wrong and bad, yet I trusted Doug. He was my hero, my best friend, so this must be okay.

"After all, I have always been different," I told myself to rationalize away any doubts.

The older I got, the more confused and warped my thinking became. I considered myself a good person, one who tried to do my best and excel at what I put my energies into. Yet, the emotions I had for Doug continued to be constantly overshadowed by a nagging sense of wrong-doing. My overwhelming need for him was so ever present that I pushed any doubts aside and continued to trust blindly in his judgment.

By the time I turned sixteen or seventeen, however, it was clear that I was fully invested in living a lie. I would hang around the Adams home as though I was part of the family, but Doug and I had our own private secret. Whenever we were left alone in the basement, even if it was only for a few moments, he used the opportunity for sexual advances. A small window at the top of the wall led to the outside and the basement steps began on the exterior of the home next to that window. Doug could see anyone coming because there would be a shadow from the feet and lower legs of the person getting ready to descend the steps to enter the basement door. It was almost always his wife. In the basement, and at every stolen opportunity, I played the role

Doug wanted, that of a best friend, incestuous daughter, and semi-innocent lover.

Over time, the sexual relationship between us had escalated. It was really sick, and yet I found it exciting, too. There were times I would be eating with his family, and he would sit across the table from me, secretively rubbing his sock-clad foot up and down my leg. If we were alone in the basement, Doug would show me the outline of his erection (his self-nicknamed "Big Angus") through his pants, sometimes revealing it altogether. As time went on, he began to coax me to touch him. The next step was to stand behind me as we played pool, pressing and rubbing his stiff member against my backside as he touched my breasts, felt between my legs, and on occasion stimulated me to orgasm. Once he pressed me to perform oral sex on him and, though it was not to the point of climax, he still enjoyed spreading juices on my face with his hands. Right before I graduated, he finally crossed that final, inevitable boundary. He'd stolen my innocence years before, but Doug eventually took my virginity on an old, hard kitchen table in his basement when I came home on vacation from college. What should have been a special experience in my development as a young woman was nothing more than a hastily and clumsily donned condom from his wallet, a few moments of equally clumsy intercourse, a guttural groan, and not even the slightest demonstration of affection. Even as I write this, consciously changing his name to protect his identity, I realize with a touch of irony that I am giving him more consideration than he ever truly gave me.

A normal 18-year-old typically looks forward to going to college, living on their own, dating and enjoying the fun and excitement of that time of life. Thanks to Doug, I was far from normal. I had earned a basketball scholarship to the University of North Carolina (UNC), and being away from home and Doug was the best thing for me. I was emotionally immature, didn't have a good sense of myself, and was challenged with a new lifestyle that included classes, weight training, basketball practice and athletic study hall in the evenings. My relationship with Doug had seriously messed up my head, and basketball games, both away and at home, only compounded my anxieties about being different. I knew I didn't feel right (whatever "right" was) but I couldn't let anyone know, especially my proud parents and neighbors who were impressed by my basketball scholarship. I felt I had to dig down deep, be mature, and not let anyone down. Everyone thought I was great, except me.

Reflecting on my four years of college, I can honestly say that I can't remember one single moment where I didn't feel a certain level of anxiety. If I was lucky, which wasn't often, it was low-grade and I could successfully ignore it. Most of the time it was moderate, but it frequently rose to an intensity that was unbearable. I was depressed most of the time, and nerves constantly knotted my stomach. I stayed so busy studying to avoid failure and practicing basketball that I simply did not have time to fall apart. This saved me from completely going under. UNC basketball wasn't all bad. In fact, it probably forced me to grow as a person and helped save me. To survive, I had to learn discipline, to broaden my views and accept others as they are. I had to make myself learn how to relate to others my own age, since there are relatively few adults in a college town. Being away from home gave me the opportunity to take a step back and gain a little perspective on my life at home. Every small step of independence I managed caused me to feel a tiny bit better about myself.

The basketball practices were very demanding. Coach Jennifer Alley made sure we were in top condition so we could survive the rigors of highly intense games. Our practices always contained a number of conditioning drills, but I hated the "suicide" the most. We had to do a series of non-stop sprints from the baseline to the free throw line, to the baseline to the half court line, back to the baseline to the free throw line at the far end of the court, back to the baseline and finally, to the baseline on the far end of the court to the baseline where the drill started. This drill was aptly named "suicide" for a good reason.

"Spread out on the baseline," Coach Alley shouted at the end of practice. "Thirty-second suicides! Everyone must make it under 30 seconds, or everyone runs it again."

Now I had a decent jump shot and could read the court well during a game, but I was not known for being fast on my feet. I would run those 30-second suicides alongside my teammates, but no matter how fast I went and how hard I tried to make the goal, more often than not I was a second or two behind it. This did not make the other girls very happy.

They knew I tried my best to make it, but that didn't help

when we were all hot, exhausted and thirsty.

"Get your ass in gear, Meredith!" they shouted at me as I brought up the rear yet again.

With everything else I was dealing with then, this was the least of my worries.

Photo by Danny Dunn

Me taking a double pump shot in a game against Wake Forest. No air under my feet!

Sometime during my early college years, I wrote this poem. I think it describes how disconnected I felt with others.

Back and forth,
Two points on a jumper
The meal is down
The books are open
But who knows the heart?

It's night now – quiet and still,
A few cars go by
People going about in
Their own corners –
Playing their games,
Looking for two –
But who knows the heart?
What it is that you see,
Might not really be me.
So look a little closer…
Because it takes someone special
To know the heart.

I could have gotten a better start on my road to recovery while I was away at college if it hadn't been for one thing: the letters. Doug, and sometimes even his wife, Betty, would write to me. The letters always sounded parental, and I guess Betty's were, in a sick way, since I always suspected that she knew and enabled her husband's activities with me. But I knew why Doug wrote and could read between his lines; he was feeling anxious about me being away from him and no longer under his influence.

What helped me most over those four years at college were my parents. Even though they had no idea what I was going through, they were always there for me, despite the distance I felt when I first went to school. Countless times they'd get in the car after work and make the long drive to watch me play. They'd bring cookies or cakes for me to share with my teammates. It was a two-and-a-half hour drive from Lynchburg to Chapel Hill, and my parents made that trek for almost every home game during the four years I played. Mom was rushing to get ready to leave to make one particular home game and was too busy to finish making a dessert that I would share with the team after the game.

"Your dad helped me make Mississippi Mud Pie this time," my mom said, laughing. "He didn't know what to do with the marshmallows, so he pushed each one down into the chocolate icing with his fingers."

"Are you kidding?" I said incredulously. "No way!"

Dad never cooked or baked anything, ever. The only time he spent in the kitchen was to eat a meal or grab a snack. He was the fix-it guy around the house and Mom was the master of the kitchen, so it was hard to believe Dad jumped gender lines to help get the dessert ready to take to me and my teammates. We had a good laugh about this Mississippi Mud Pie experience. Our relationship began to heal.

Every time I'd run out onto the court for pre-game warm-ups, Dad would blast out his familiar whistle, (the same one he used to call me home when I was a child playing in the neighborhood) that signaled that he and Mom were there. I finally realized how much they loved me, but felt confused and sad, unable to share my problems with them. 'They would never understand,' I thought, so I just tried even harder to appear strong and confident.

Sometimes, despite my efforts, they could tell I was unhappy, but I led them to believe it was my demanding schedule. In reality, it was because I felt empty inside, like the wind was blowing straight through me. I couldn't confide how miserable I was, because I didn't yet have a workable way to express those thoughts or to deal with reality. The years I needed to grow up, mature, and prepare myself for college had been short circuited, and my emotional growth had been warped and stifled.

With each passing year, my problems and anxiety only seemed to increase. Fear gripped my brain every waking moment: fear of the future; fear of the present; fear of everything. I felt increasingly disconnected from my surroundings, as though I was floating away, a feeling so horrible that it's very difficult to put it into words even now. I was detached from my environment and the people around me, and I experienced the terror of being totally alone. The level of anxiety I experienced then was extremely intense, verging on constant panic.

One day, I got a letter from Doug that really sent me over the edge. I don't remember anything unusual in it, but perhaps I had reached the point where I couldn't stand the guilt and shame any longer. I took that letter to the woods off the edge of campus where an old stone building stood, abandoned and secluded. I remember the dry leaves blowing on the ground in the cool breeze. I took a match and set the letter afire and fell to my knees as it burned, as if begging to somehow cleanse myself from that man and all my dreadful guilt. I hated and blamed myself for what had been done in his basement all that time. I wanted God to forgive me and relieve me from the mental agony I was suffering. For that brief moment while the letter burned, there was a momentary sense of relief, but when nothing was left but a few black ashes, I was still there…and so was the pain.

The mental anguish got so bad that I feared losing my mind. I remember sitting in a large classroom with stadium seating. I can still clearly recall what the professor looked like: big, overweight, and slovenly. My mind sped at a million miles an hour and I was unable to make it stop. It spun faster and faster out of control, until my mind floated above my body. I couldn't even hear the professor speaking. I could only see this big blob down front, and a mouth moving soundlessly. I knew I had gone over the edge.

I went to the library to try to study for a big test, and I must have been sitting there for hours looking at the same page, never even seeing it. I couldn't cry. I couldn't scream. I couldn't escape it. The terror overtook and consumed my mind, body and soul.

In the old gymnasium at UNC, where a lot of students went to play pick-up basketball, there was a ladies' lounge that had a worn green leather couch right next to the doorway. Whenever I was really in bad shape and too far away from the shelter of my dorm, I'd stop by this lounge and lie on that old couch, looking up at the ceiling, seeing nothing. I wonder if anyone in the parade of women who came in to use the rest room noticed me, day after day, wallowing there, trying to rest and collect my thoughts. That old couch became my refuge, my escape from the world when I had an hour or so after class before basketball practice. It eventually became a part of my daily routine and a way to try to sort through my feelings while readying myself for a mentally and physically demanding practice.

Looking back now, I realize that I must have a remarkably high level of inner strength to have dealt with so much trauma without totally cracking up. Instead I plodded along day by day, never missing a practice or game and keeping my grades at a B average, while inside I was unmistakably miserable. I had wild mood swings and feelings that were unreal as I desperately read and searched the Bible for some truth, some bits of wisdom that would free my mind from the pain. I read the New Testament, and when I got to the eighth chapter of John, I finally found something that spoke to me in a very real way. This chapter talked of scribes and Pharisees bringing to Jesus a woman who had been caught in the act of adultery. They felt she should be stoned for her tremendous sin as the Mosaic Law demanded. But Jesus, stooping down while running his fingers through the sand as though he didn't hear them, wisely listened in silence. When they pressed the issue, he stood up and said, "He that is without sin among you, let him first cast a stone at her." Each man searched his own soul, and one by one they walked away, realizing that they had committed sins in their own lives too, even if it was something other than adultery.

This chapter in the Bible made me realize that although what had happened between me and Doug was sinful and wrong, it was not any worse than other sins. We are all sinners. This concept lifted my burden a tiny bit and gave me hope at last. If Jesus forgave this woman, he'd forgive me, as he does all sinners. The real trick then became learning how to forgive myself, and that did not happen overnight.

I finally decided that I would have to talk about my problems with someone if I was ever going to be able to cope. That person was Aprille Shaffer, a teammate on the basketball team. Our point guard and a very talented player, she was quick, energetic and a great defensive player and outside shooter. She ran the court with authority and seemed to possess a high level of confidence and determination. I confided in Aprille, who was as supportive and caring as any person could have been, a true friend who listened and hurt for me. It didn't come to her as any surprise that I had some big problems; the whole team had seen that and felt powerless to help me.

At that time, I really had no other choice but to seek out a confidant if I wanted to maintain my sanity. We have to hit rock bottom before finally realizing that some problems are bigger than ourselves. In order to heal, or even survive, we have to reach out for help. I was finally at that point. Thoughts of suicide had entered my mind because every waking moment was filled with intense anxiety and dread. I needed relief, and

I needed it soon if I was going to continue living.

The quickest way to get immediate relief from the agony would be to kill myself, I reasoned, but I also knew there was no turning back from that act. Once you're dead, you are dead. I was afraid of what would happen to my soul if I took my own life. I didn't have a clear picture of hell. I felt perhaps I was already living in my own hell, but wasn't willing to risk that after death it could be many times worse, for all eternity.

I had always prided myself on being able to deal with tough things, in my ability to dig deep, suck it up and forge on. I felt like suicide would be a cop-out, a coward's solution, and I couldn't bear thinking of myself in those terms. What would suicide do to my family and friends? How would that make them feel? I shouldered the entire responsibility for my problems and felt like I needed to suffer to pay for all those years I had sneaked around in Doug's basement. Although I did not know what was in store for me, somehow I hoped my life would have a purpose one day. Telling Aprille about my secret sins marked the first baby step toward recovering from years of emotional and sexual abuse and fulfilling that purpose.

At that time, I didn't even understand that I had been abused. You hear or read about abuse that happens to other people. It would take years to finally admit that I had been abused, thanks to countless sessions with therapists and hard work examining my inner self. My mental files had been corrupted by Doug's abuse, and I needed to re-program my mind in a more healthy way. Opening up to

Aprille cracked the door to mental health for me. Because she was kind, receptive and supportive, I was able to start walking away from my past.

For the rest of my senior year, Aprille was my best and only true friend. I had other friends both on and off the team and they cared about me to a degree, but Aprille was the only person at school who really knew me. She couldn't crawl inside my brain and straighten things out or remove the fear, anxiety, guilt and depression, but she could listen and try to understand. Countless times I turned to her when I knew she didn't really have time to listen, but not once did she turn me away. At one point she gave me a gift that touched me deeply. It was a tan and white earthenware container with the words, "Unlimited Potential" on it and a big cork lid inserted at the top. Inside were a number of small paper scrolls, each tied with a narrow gold ribbon. Every scroll contained a different positive saying, an affirmative quote or snippet of wisdom. Aprille had painstakingly made each one of these for me by hand, filling the container with hope. I opened one every morning after that to help me start my day out right. Thanks to Aprille and her unique and patient friendship, I made it through senior year with my B average and sanity intact.

***

The only memory I have of my father is him fighting with my mom on the very last night I saw him. I was four years old, and I remember my baby sister, Bernice, my older brother, Willie, and me and my mom came home one night, and my dad was sitting in the dark in the living room. As soon as she walked into the apartment, he started arguing with my mom. They both went into the bedroom fighting and that is the only thing I remember about my dad. A few weeks later we were going to his funeral. I never told my mother I remembered anything from that night, but when I got older she told me what really happened. She said that my dad was up drinking and thought that we all came home too late. He thought she was out cheating on him and they got into a big fight. She said that he beat her up pretty bad, but she managed to grab my brother and sister and me and run to my cousin's apartment.

A couple of weeks later, the police found my dad dead. They said it was suicide, but deep down inside I always felt that somebody killed my dad. I do believe I told my mom that my last memory of my dad was that night she left and they had that fight, my only memory really. And the funeral, I was like, four, and I remember we were at my dad's funeral and we were at the cemetery and I remember she cried and how hard she squeezed my hand. Those are the only two memories I have.

Growing up in a single-parent home had its ups and downs. A year or two after my dad died, my mom was in a car accident. She was traveling with some friends and was hit head on by a drunk driver. She spent almost a year in the hospital and Willie, Bernice and I had to live with my aunt. The whole time I stayed with my aunt I thought my mom was going to die. I only saw her once when she was in the hospital and she looked worse than what I'd pictured. She had tubes in her nose and stitches in her forehead. Her hip and leg were broken and she had her leg in some kind of sling. Seeing my mom like that made me even more afraid. I felt like I just lost my dad and now my mom was going to die too. Everybody in my family was talking about who was going to take care of us and this made the whole situation worse. Eventually my mom got better and got out of the hospital. She took the money she got from the accident and put a down payment on a house in a nice, middle-class neighborhood.

At this time in my life I was about eight years old, Willie was 12 and Bernice was five. My mom had to work two jobs just to pay the bills and put food on the table. So, my brother Willie used to watch me and my sister which meant we did what we wanted to do. Me and Willie got into a lot of fights with the neighborhood kids and at school. Someone would make a comment about my dad, and I always felt like since he was dead they had no right to talk about him. Mom would always sit me down and tell me that was no reason to fight and what people said about my dad and her couldn't hurt them. Mom always tried to make up for the time she missed with us but she would be too tired when she got off from work. I never got upset over this because I knew Mom wanted to be with us, and she always told us how much we meant to her.

One thing we all did together was go to church. Even if I didn't want to go, Mom made me go. I thought church was the most boring thing in the world. I would try to listen to the Preacher preach and always ended up falling asleep. Mom would pinch me so hard that it would bring tears to my eyes. The church we went to, the people who went there were well off. Meredith's boss, the publisher of the newspaper, went there. The church gave my mom a lot of support during those years. I remember sometimes we didn't have any food in the house and Mom would talk to one of the deacons of the church and as soon as church was over they would have a couple of bags of food for us. I always was embarrassed carrying the bags to the car. We were always grateful, but I still hated walking out with a bag of food. Everybody at the church was upper-class people and I didn't want them to know that we were poor. We might not have been dirt poor, but we were poor.

Chapter 3
Homecoming

I returned to Lynchburg after graduating from UNC. I got a job at my hometown newspaper and started my first of what would be five years of intensive counseling. I took it very seriously and showed up on time for every session with Dr. Dan Glenn, a psychologist. He was a thin, pale man in his fifties who always seemed depressed to me. Perhaps aided by that, he helped open my mind and emotions as I shared and listened. Dr. Glenn helped me to recognize how disastrous all those years with Doug were to my personal development, and how that time in my life negatively impacted my self-esteem, even my identity. He helped me to work through all of the misplaced negative feelings I had toward my father. The therapy sessions made me face some hard truths about myself and gave me tools to start understanding who I truly am. The work was long and tortuous, and I have saved notebooks filled with statements like "I love myself," written over and over again in an attempt to internalize these affirmations. I still experienced crippling anxiety, and at one time suffered from panic attacks, but I kept on fighting for my peace and sanity.

Over time, Dr. Glenn realized that there was more going on with me than behavioral therapy alone could tackle. He referred me to Dr. Amos Yen, a psychiatrist, and my work continued with him. After several months of seeing Dr. Yen, I was diagnosed with bipolar disorder, and he started me on 450 mg of Lithium, twice a day. Within three weeks I felt much more normal and my family was astounded at the changes they saw in me. Depression, irritability, sadness and mood swings gave way to a calmness my family had never seen. Small irritations would escalate before. Now, those same irritations would dissipate, sliding away like raindrops on a window.

Dr. Glenn and Dr. Yenn had given me some tools to use in my pursuit of mental health, some less than conventional. Whenever negative thoughts would enter my mind, I'd employ another, stronger thought.

"Fuck it."

No kidding. Those are the two words that came to mind, and I have no idea why. Maybe that's how lithium works for me! With proper medication, I suddenly had more control that allowed my mind to release the problem thought, putting me on a healthy course. Nearly 40 years later, I still take the same daily dosage of Lithium and I still see a counselor, albeit far less frequently. People who won't take their medicine because it interferes with their creativity, or because they miss the manic part of the disease mystify me.

I couldn't live with all of that self-induced drama, and for me, Lithium doesn't eliminate creativity or mania, it simply dials it backwards to a more tolerable level.

I know what I write here may sound like I have simplified things, but believe me, therapy was anything but simple. In *The Road Less Traveled* by M. Scott Peck, he wrote about neural pathways being created in the human mind. Repetitive thoughts, Peck says, literally wear grooves in your brain, and the way to improve your life is to change your patterns of thinking from negative to positive thoughts. If I wanted to be a better person, I had to think of myself differently. I had to somehow start thinking about different things, or the same things in a different, more positive way, if I wanted to leave old ways and develop new ones. It was immensely difficult, but, little by little, I made progress.

On the advice of Dr. Yen, I also attended a helpful therapy group that met in the evenings, Adults Molested As Children (AMAC). At the time, the meetings were held in a small room on the ground floor of Virginia Baptist Hospital in Lynchburg. On Thursday evenings we sat in a circle so we could see each other and conversation would be easier. During the first sessions, each person was given the opportunity to talk about their past experiences and their reasons for joining the group. After that, we were given time to talk about our progress or to ask the group for input on any issues. There were almost always 12 to 15 people there, and after hearing what others said about their own molestations, I recall realizing that there were a lot of really sick people out there in the world.

I continued reading my Bible, mostly the New Testament because it was easier for me to understand. Not only was I full of guilt and remorse, I was distraught at the thought that I might never rid myself of that pain. Scripture helped me to begin to forgive myself, but it took a long time for me to release those horrid feelings.

I came to some conclusions about God and what I believed. I had clarity and it was simple: I believe we must live in the truth. We may be able to deceive other people, but we can't fool ourselves and we most certainly cannot fool God. He has created us in His image, so it is on us to do our best to live up to His expectations to become Christ like, like Him. We will never get there this side of heaven, but we honor Him when we try. It's a simple way of experiencing life, but it reduces drama and bad situations and causes me to tap into my higher self.

I don't know anyone who could fully understand the impact that Doug's abuse and a diagnosis of Bipolar Disorder had on my life. It made me question many things about myself, but it also pushed me to become a better person and leave behind an honorable legacy. I decided to volunteer for BBBS to fill my free time with positivity, but it was much more than that. I often wondered how my life would have turned out if Doug had been a good influence in my life, a true mentor instead of a selfish, monstrous pervert. I decided that I was ready to be a good influence in someone's life, and that someone was Darrin. Was this decision in part an attempt at expiation of my own lingering guilt? I don't know, but I learned fairly quickly that Darrin was destined to be someone good for my life, too.

***

I had no clue that Meredith had issues or took medicine or anything like that. She didn't show it; she didn't treat me any different. She was always nice to me. Later, when she told me she suffered from bipolar, I didn't know it. I didn't know what it was at first, really. But I never felt she had something going on or something was bothering her. I never had a clue. She was always good to me, she was never mean. Well, the time she didn't take me to Smith Mountain Lake when we were supposed to ride the jet ski I always thought she was teaching me a lesson, but she might have just been being mean to me! But when we first met, I had no clue about what had gone on with Meredith. For a long time I didn't know. I know more now, but back then she never went in to like great detail about what happened. She hinted that some things happened to her when she was younger and she didn't want kids to have to deal with that. But I never sensed it with her with the way she acted or the way she treated me. I think she shared with me just as part of our bonding, it wasn't like a lesson that you need to watch out for older people or anything like that. She made sure I knew there were some messed up people out there. Some people are screwed up, was the message. But she never warned me to beware or not trust people or anything.

***

I started driving over to Fairview Heights each week to pick up my Little Brother, Darrin. During those early months I would go in and visit with Patricia for a minute, if she was home. She seemed to like me and she trusted me with her son. I was trying to establish a strong comfort level with her and wanted to put her at ease about my giving her son some experiences that he'd never had before. When a kid grows up in a single parent home where the mom is working a lot of hours to make ends meet, taking expensive vacations or even enjoying entertainment around town are unimagined luxuries.

The King family.

I never thought, I got a mom I don't need another. My mom worked two or three different jobs and she stayed busy. She didn't have time to do things with us, but we saw that as normal too. And then Will raised us. I mean, she had two jobs, so Will was the babysitter, the big brother, and that was part of life. We knew a lot of other families like that. When I got older, I realized it must have been hard, because I'd come back and talk about Meredith like she was the greatest thing since sliced bread. We did this and she got me this and got me that. I know mom wished she could do some of those things. But she never came out and said anything, never said anything bad about Meredith. I think she wanted to do those things, but she understood it was nice for me to be able to do those things on top of a good way for me to stay out of trouble. I was getting into football and stuff like that. I think she recognized it was good for me. She and Meredith, in my memory, only had one issue and that was with Will. Will sold drugs when he was a teenager, so he always had extra money and would get me stuff with the money. One time I had on a pair of hundred dollar tennis shoes, and Meredith told me I shouldn't be wearing them. I went home and told my mom that Meredith said they were bought with drug money, and my mom wasn't too happy about that. Aside from that incident, they always got along.

There were strong females in my life besides my mom. My aunt Nancy was my mom's younger sister, then I had my grandfather's sister, my great aunt, Aunt Barb, who was more like a grandmother because she used to come and spoil all of us, including my mom. But Nancy, we grew up with them so they were like brothers and sisters. One time my Grandfather was arguing with grandmother, my mom's mom, and he had a gun but wasn't pointing at her really but they started wrestling with it and at one point he pulled back hard and my uncle Steve was right behind my grandfather and it hit Steve in the head really hard and that's what kind of messed him up, then the gun went off and killed my grandmom.

When my grandad went to prison, my mom, Patricia, the

oldest, took in Steve, Nancy, Bob, and Richard with us and my mom raised them too. Nancy was second oldest, then Bob, then Richard, then Steve. We were all close, but Will was real close with Richard and me and Steve were really close. Steve wouldn't talk a lot with people, wouldn't do much, for the longest time. But at night we'd hear him running around in the house in the middle of the night while everybody was asleep and talking, but he wouldn't talk to anybody else for the longest time. They were more like brothers and sisters than aunts and uncles. I didn't necessarily see Nancy as my aunt, she was always like a big sister but now that she's older, she's 50 now I see my mom in her, my mom never made it that far, she died at 39, but I see Nancy now and I see she's similar and she's my mom's sister and I have a lot of respect for her and everything she's been through. She is kinda like the matriarch of the family now, but Nancy is, like, quieter, she takes a lot without saying anything, where my mom, she was sweet and nice, but if you said the wrong thing or if you did something, she was going to let you know.

My grandfather wasn't away for long. I was close to my grandad. I was his favorite. For the longest time I was the youngest grandchild. So, I got to ride on the tractor with him when he planted the fields. He took me everywhere with him. I was his shadow. When my brother and all the others were picking on me, I would go with him. He had no problem showing favorites. This was after he came out, before that I was too young to know. I mean, my mom told us what happened, but he was always good to me. He was a farmer, and he worked for an Oldsmobile company. I remember him putting on a uniform and going to work, but he was a farmer mostly. He planted crops and sold his crops. I have a lot of memories of us going to his house.

I didn't understand at the time, but I might ask my uncle, (my great uncle, my grandmothers brother) a question about my grandad cause my grandfather was my world. Even though I brought it up, I never saw or realized he might hate him. He never said anything in my presence bad about him. My mom explained it to me when I was older and then it finally clicked on me who they were and who they are in the dynamics of it.

***

When I took Darrin to a local mall for the first time, we had a great time wandering around the different stores. I don't think he had ever been there. We developed a favorite dining spot there; Giovanni's Pizza served up the largest, sloppiest pizzas I had ever seen. Neither of us was shy when it came to eating, and we would wipe out a large pizza, grease and all. At the mall, video games, mostly Pac Man and fighting games like karate, were big at the time. I learned early on that Darrin had good hand–eye coordination, and he almost always won the kicking games. I have to admit, one of the nice things about having a kid in your life is that it gives you license to act like a kid again, too. The mall was a pretty consistent favorite, but in the years ahead of us we did many other things together. I bought a house in Forest, Virginia when I was 27, so there were plenty of things to do there.

It wasn't long before the local television station wanted to do a story on us, since the match between a female and a male was so unusual. They followed us with their cameras in the mall, while we ate pizza, and at my house while Darrin drove a remote control car in the driveway. Neither of us cared much for that exposure. We did it for BBBS. We were happy hanging out together and finding ways to have fun.

I always tried to make sure that Darrin didn't just see me as someone to have fun with, but as someone who could also teach him life principles. When I first bought my home, the kitchen wallpaper featured big, ugly flowers. One day, Darrin and I decided to tackle taking that awful wallpaper down. I gave him a chair to stand on and together we figured out how to remove it. It took time, but we got the job done, giving us both a sense of shared accomplishment.

***

Tearing down old ugly wallpaper in my kitchen.

It showed me a new and different lifestyle. I was living in the moment and happy to be there. I never thought one life was better than another life, even going to her home, I just enjoyed going there. I wasn't there for the house, I was there for her. And the cookies. And the pancakes. I thought Meredith was the best cook in the world! Pancakes and cookies, what else do you need?

I loved both of her parents. Her mother was super sweet to me. I never saw any other side of her. Her dad was always nice to me and I always thought he was, like a military guy, very straight, and it was always yes sir, yes sir. But he was still very nice and kind.

Throwing the football, playing basketball, Meredith kind of really got me into sports. She told me she played basketball and she knew Michael Jordan and that was all I needed from that day, I was like, okay. And she could play and she could shoot. She was making shot after shot and mine was all over the place, so I knew. The proof was in the pudding. I had played around a little but I actually threw the football with her more than anybody else. I had my brother and some backyard football but besides that I didn't have anybody I threw the football with except Meredith. Meredith and my mom both got me into football. I loved football, and basketball. I liked basketball but didn't follow it really. I knew who Michael Jordan was, but Meredith actually watched it and I started watching it with her. And then she played for North Carolina and we watched them and North Carolina became my basketball team. Still are. Stuff like that.

We played video games. That was a big deal, pizza, and video games, pizza and video games. And then she got me into studying. Once she found out my grades were lackluster. She got me to spell her name. It was the first time I had heard the name Meredith any way and she's like "spell my name." I'm going, "M-U-D..." and she says, "We're going to work on this." And eventually she got me to spell her name out. So, it wasn't only pizza and stuff. She threw some education in there and hitting the books. Like I said, my mom had two or three jobs and she didn't have the time to check on me "you do your homework?" "Yeah, I did my homework" and that was it. So my grades were slipping. Got out of elementary school and got into middle school and my grades were low. So, Meredith got me into studying. I don't know how Meredith found out. I guess my mom saw my grades and was like "What?" and she told Meredith. Like I said, I couldn't spell her name so she got me to do that. She gave me incentives.

One time I got straight As, I think in sixth grade. Before that I had like Cs and Ds. But I wasn't applying myself. She told me if I got straight As she'd get me this Transformer that was popular at the time, Optimus Prime. It was the new Transformer. It was the leader of the Transformers, and I had to have it. So, this time I tried. I got almost all As but two Bs. But the next time I got all As and she got me the Transformer, which I kept for years. She got me to apply myself. There wasn't anything before pushing me to apply myself. But everything came kind of easy. At school I'd listen to the teacher and I could get by without really trying. If I could go back and change some things, I'd want to apply myself better.

*The two of us enjoying pizza
at an outdoor park in Lynchburg.*

At that time in my life, I was dating a man named Rick Stevens, the business manager for a local car dealership. We met one day at Walden Pond, an apartment complex near the newspaper where I worked. Rick rented an apartment near me during a divorce from his wife, and eventually moved into the home they had purchased together off Lakeside Drive. Rick and I found that we had a common love for playing volleyball, both indoor and outdoor. Many weekends involved tournaments in the area, and it was fun to meet new people. During this time, I received therapy but it never seemed to help my ability to trust, so I was unable to get very emotionally close to Rick. We saw each other for four years and despite his patience and caring for me, due to my ongoing issues our relationship never got past a deep friendship. Rick eventually grew more and more resentful, and I grew weary of trying.

Darrin never liked Rick, although he never said much

about it at the time. Rick was openly jealous, and saw every minute that I spent with Darrin as a minute I could have been with him instead. It was easier for me to be with Darrin as a Big Sister, and more difficult to be with Rick, who always wanted a deeper relationship. Rick may have been what I needed in my life at that time, but I wasn't what Rick needed. Looking at that time in my life, I realize that maybe he should have made the decision to move on sooner.

***

I didn't dislike him [Rick]. He wasn't mean to me, I just didn't connect with him. One instance when we went to Busch Gardens or the beach or somewhere and we came back to the house I was like half asleep and I got out of the car and said goodnight. Like the next time I saw him he told me I should be more thankful. It wasn't that he said that, it was the way he said it, and took hold of my arm while he said it. He hadn't built any relationship with me where he might talk to me that way. Meredith knew I appreciated it. I always appreciated what she did for me and she knew. He never threw the football with me, I don't think, and he didn't bother me or with me, we just didn't connect. We went to Busch Gardens once and I won this big dragon. I had that dragon hanging on my wall for about 15 years. It was a crossbow game and you had to aim it and shoot the target. I got it on the first try, but I think the only reason I got it was because Rick was like, "You gotta do it! You gotta aim it! You gotta look at what you want!" So, I jumped on it and looked at it and first shot -PSHEW- look at that!

***

I continued to see Darrin, but structured our relationship so that I could develop consistent expectations for him. If Darrin asked me for money for something he wanted, I would find work around the house that he could do to earn it instead of just giving it to him. He tested me a couple of times as kids will do, but after that didn't work, he learned to say, "Can I wash your car or cut the grass for some money?" Of course, that only applied to extra things Darrin wanted. Our adventures together, a movie, or pizza and video games, were still happily paid for by me.

Darrin was never a whiney kid. I never saw him restless or bored. Sometimes he was quiet, but most of the time he was "all in." When we were at my house, we would bake cookies together and stuff ourselves with cookie dough. Since I had always been an athlete and had played backyard football when I was a kid, I could hold my own throwing passes to Darrin in my yard. I didn't throw perfect spirals all of the time, and neither did he, but we were both good enough to run and juke and hit each other with a pass on the move. Occasionally, we would even build a fire in a natural part of my front yard and make S'mores. Neighbors would drive by, possibly wondering what the heck we were doing building a fire in the front yard, but we didn't care. We were happy to spend the time together, getting sticky marshmallows and melted chocolate all over our hands and faces.

Sometimes Darrin and I spent time at his house. Patricia was generally there or on her way home from her work at Central Virginia Training Center. They lived in a ranch house, mostly brick, with ample space for Darrin and his brother, Will, and sister, Bernice. You could tell the kitchen was a place where they spent a fair amount of time. One cabinet door was loose and hanging by its hinge, the oven was in need of a good cleaning and the walls could stand painting, but when a single mom works two jobs, those things are not a priority.

When Darrin needed help with homework, we'd sit at the kitchen table together and do arithmetic, or I'd call out spelling words. Before starting, I'd tell him he would have to spell my name correctly before we could tackle his classwork. The first time, I spelled out M-e-r-e-d-i-t-h for him. By the third session, Darrin could easily spell my name and most of his spelling words. Darrin was smart, and the only thing that could keep him from being a high achiever was his fondness for clowning around in class and his occasional fights. Even though he was still pretty small, he had wide shoulders and was not one to retreat from another boy. His mischief making would also get him into trouble with a teacher every now and then.

At one time, the family acquired a little dog with white, curly hair, which I only saw a couple of times before it was gone.

"Hey, Darrin, what happened to that little fuzzy white dog you had?" I asked.

"We don't have it any more," Darrin said flatly.

I thought perhaps they had given it away, or maybe it had run off.

"What happened to it?" I said.

"It was on a chain and fell off the deck and hung himself."

That was the first time I saw that Darrin could shove his hurt way down inside, something he may have learned to do as a little boy when his father died.

***

I internalize everything. I mean, if something bothered me or was eating on my mind, I don't think I showed it. I've got a habit or way of pushing things in the back of my mind, I guess. Sometimes things can be going on and maybe I can get distracted with the other stuff and not think about that, I can do that easily. That's with everything. I mean, I've done that with a lot of things, when my mom died, when she was sick, all types of stuff. Just push it to the back of my mind or focus on something else or keep busy or whatever. I don't let it dominate my thoughts.

That was the way it was. We had had that dog for a little while. She died. She fell off the porch and hung herself. I was devastated that day. I didn't want to go to school or whatever. My mom said get up and go to school. That day I might have thought about it that whole day but after that day, I gotta move on. We had dogs before that didn't work out that she actually took away, like, we can't keep this dog, and we'd come home and the dog would be gone. You got a little sad but there ain't no boo hoo hoo. It's just the way we came up. I felt bad that I left her on the deck, with a leash on, tied up. I still can't imagine to this day how she jumped off the porch. It was like a ten foot high deck. But when I woke up she was just hanging there, when I opened the back door to go out she was hanging there. I was tore up about that. I thought it was my fault.

***

Darrin and I went on outings to the skating rink, often taking a few of his friends so they could all skate together. The kids always had fun at my favorite childhood skating rink on Old Graves Mill Road. They'd go speeding around the wood floors and then zip off for a soda or snack and return to the skate floor. I was a much more conservative skater than when I was as a child, but I still enjoyed it. One time, Darrin wanted to go skating but the rink we always went to was closed. I told Darrin there was one in nearby New London, and we could go there. When we arrived, Darrin got his skates, laced them up, and hit the floor. As I watched from the sidelines, I noticed Darrin was the only black kid there, and every time one of those privileged white kids would pass Darrin, they would either bump, shove, or trip him. It took several falls before I was certain that I was witnessing Darrin's first encounter with overt racism. I think it took all of his courage not to cry until I got him out of there and safely in the car. We talked about what had happened, and that some of those kids must have missed some valuable guidance somewhere in their young lives. I tried to help him understand prejudice, even though I had a hard time understanding it myself. I told him that not everyone is like that, and encouraged Darrin to follow Dr. Martin Luther King's advice, to judge people by the content of their character, not by the color of their skin. I think he understood.

***

Darrin at the newspaper where I worked.

That was my first real experience with racism. At least that I recognized. Even at our church, where we were one of only two black families, they all were nice and friendly. No one treated us different. But I never had anyone pushing me or being mean to me out of spite. They were tripping me and pushing me down and whatever but at the time I'm like whatever I'm just gonna get up and keep skating. I don't think I figured they were doing it to me because I was a black kid. But when I look back on it, I was not bothering anybody, just skating by myself. I couldn't figure out why they kept fucking with me. Growing up in the country with my uncles and my cousins and being the youngest, I was used to being picked on and having them beat me up and fighting all the time. I was a scrapper but this was a new environment and new people so I kept it in. I got up. I wasn't going to let them see me cry. But I do remember Meredith consoling me. She recognized it, saw what was going on. We left. I can't remember exactly what she said, but I felt her put her arm around me to let me know it was going to be all right, we don't need to be here. I felt better around her. I do remember that skating port was bigger than ours, nicer, it was giant, so I do remember that. It wasn't like I built something negative or bad out of that experience it was, again, forget about it.

Meredith never embarrassed me. She was always like, the coolest thing since sliced bread. And I always told people, they'd ask, "Who is that?" "That's my big sister", and they'd be like "Big sister?! She's white and you're black?!" and I'd go "She ain't gotta be black, brother. She's my big sister." The funny thing is I tell people now, "Well, I'm gonna go see my big sister." And they say "You didn't tell me you had a big sister" and I gotta explain she's my big brothers and big sisters sister. I gotta break it into detail, explaining Meredith to other people.

***

There were also times I'd take Darrin to work with me for short visits where I might be checking on work, or talking with an employee about a concern that needed my attention. He loved sitting at my desk and messing around on my computer. The folks I worked with genuinely liked Darrin. They'd stop by, talk to him and show him how things worked. I was at The News & Advance then, a daily newspaper serving Lynchburg and the surrounding counties. I had a lot of different jobs over the fourteen years I worked there. I went from advertising salesperson, to sales manager; then to creative director; and eventually, advertising director. Newspapers are interesting places, and I liked taking Darrin to the press room, especially if a paper was printing and he could see it come off the press. My different positions allowed me to show Darrin many sides to the business while unknowingly helping me to build skills sets I would need to start a magazine many years later.

***

Her friend, Gaither, worked at the paper and he stood out, even when I first met him. I always liked him. We just clicked and we could talk. Another guy she worked with at the News and Advance, Jim Brent, he was nice. We did things at the newspaper and he showed me around. All the people I met through Meredith were nice. He's the only one I remember by name there. He stood out for being so nice, but they were all nice.

***

Thomas Road Baptist Church put together an awesome haunted house every year for Halloween, which became one of our favorite traditions. It was held in an old, abandoned house near the downtown area. There was a tremendous amount of effort put into making the event multi-faceted and entertaining, not to mention scary. The folks who worked the haunted house were professionally dressed and made up to be as frightfully spooky as possible. When we entered the haunted house, they directed us down a long corridor that got narrower and narrower as we moved along. By the end of it, we could barely squeeze out of the corridor. Skeletons and other scary creatures would jump out at random places, and it was so dark we could hardly tell where we were going. Darrin loved it, and I must admit it appealed to the childlike part of me, too. We went for several years until it closed. The fun never got old.

Our outings weren't all fun and games, though. I was

always looking for those teachable moments.

Darrin and I had a reason to talk about the importance of telling the truth one day when he and a friend were shooting basketball on a neighbor's hoop. The neighbor wasn't home and I didn't realize they were using his goal located on the cul de sac behind me. Darrin came running home to my house.

"It wasn't my fault! I hit the pole with my shoulder and it broke and the goal came crashing down!" he said.

I went to inspect the damage and knew right away that the explanation Darrin gave me was not what happened.

"Darrin, tell me again. How did this pole come down?"

"We were shooting, and I ran toward the goal and my shoulder hit the pole and it came down," Darrin responded.

I looked at the damage and remained silent. We walked over to my house and sat down on the back deck.

"Darrin, you and I both know that the pole did not break from your shoulder hitting it," I said, after some thought.

Darrin said nothing, trying to figure out which way to go. Saying nothing neither confirmed nor denied.

"So, I'm thinking that the pole was most likely broken from someone hanging on the rim. And I'm thinking that person was you," I said, looking intently at him. It was a rusty old pole and the goal had been set lower than the normal height of 10 feet, a real temptation for youngsters to try to dunk. Darrin stuck stubbornly to his story for a bit, but eventually owned up to the truth.

"Okay, I did it. I hung on the rim," Darrin admitted. "I was hanging on it and I guess my weight was too much. I'm sorry."

We then talked about the importance of telling the truth. I went to the neighbors and told them what had happened and agreed to replace the pole and fix it, which is what I did. This one incident was so real for us, and such a good lesson. I let Darrin know that lying is for weak people and that telling the truth is a sign of strength. I had never known Darrin to embellish or sidestep the truth before. I think he learned a lesson that day, and I like to believe it was a lesson he carried forward into adulthood. Years later, we would bring up that experience and joke about how strong his shoulder must have been to knock down that pole!

***

I don't know what was going on in my head when we went and told her. We knew we were in trouble. We concocted the whole story and it would have been easier to say we were dunking and hung on the rim. You don't know how stupid your excuses are until you get older. They never worked!

Darrin and me playing cards.

When Darrin turned 13, I told him that he could take a friend along whenever he and I would be spending time together. As a teenager, I wanted him to continue to feel comfortable with me and he was at the age where he was changing and growing. From that point forward, Darrin included a friend which was almost always his cousin, Darnell McQueen, who was about his age. Darnell was an upbeat and talkative person who could talk to anyone, whether he knew them or not. He was so outgoing and charismatic that I always told him that he should get a job in sales when he grew up. The three of us had some laughs together and Darnell brought a new dimension to our excursions. It didn't matter what we did, we had a good time.

One day I told the young teenagers that we were going to have a pancake eating contest. Immediately the boys became rivals and each boasted of being able to out-eat one another. I don't think it mattered if there was a prize, they just wanted bragging rights. I haven't cooked much in my lifetime, but I can make pancakes with proficiency. I started filling their plates with large pancakes made similar in size, just to be fair. Towards the end they were groaning with each bite as I laughed and laughed. In the end, it was Darnell who beat out Darrin, but both boys were miserable for the next few hours.

About that same time one of my aunts called my mother to tell her that I needed to end my relationship with Darrin. This aunt lived in the country and had old-fashioned notions about black people. Her ignorance was due to a complete lack of socialization with anyone who was different from her. My aunt had no black friends. She worked at Peebles Department Store and perhaps interacted with black people there, but I suspect this was the extent of it. I wanted my family to be more enlightened than that, but I understood where my aunt was coming from. My mom, bless her, didn't bat an eye when her sister said that now that Darrin was 13, he was going to rape me. She had been spoiling Darrin for years with caramel cakes and other desserts and continued to love and accept him whenever she saw him.

When Darrin and Darnell were around 15 or 16, me and my sister, Ginger White, took them skiing at Wintergreen Resort. It was Christmas time, and I had gifts for them, but first they wanted to hit the slopes. Neither of them had ever been at a ski resort, much less skied. They fearlessly hit the slopes. They were the only black guys on the slopes that day and they skied straight down the beginner hill with no back and forth maneuvering for control or reduced speed. No matter how steep the path, they went straight down as fast as they could, their pants hanging off their butts, making themselves a truly different spectacle on the slopes. Unlike the skating rink experience, no one at Wintergreen seemed to mind. Darrin and Darnell were respectful of others on the slope and stayed well out of their way so as not to cause an inadvertent crash, except for one incident. Darrin couldn't avoid me. He slammed into me at high speed, then quickly turned my body, so that when we fell I would land on top of him, not vice versa. By that time,

Darrin was a pretty big fellow and I am pretty sure if he hadn't spun me around, I would have been crushed by his six-foot frame. Despite my bruises, it made me feel good that he had looked out for me and made sure I wasn't hurt.

Later that day, we went inside and got a table near a fireplace. We all ordered hot chocolate and opened gifts. I can't remember now what I had bought for them, but I'm pretty sure I spoiled them because it always made me happy, too. I probably got each of them a nice coat and a few other small items. I know I gave them some spending money because I remember they were very happy about that. There were others in the lodge that day who were enjoying their wine and cocktails and looking at two black kids with two white women, watching our time together, but I didn't care. Their glances didn't stop us at all, Ginger included, from having a great time. I really loved those kids, and while I tried hard not to spoil them most of the time, I felt like Christmas was the season where I could really give without guilt.

***

I loved it! I keep saying I want to do it now, but all I can think about now is falling. The only time I went, we went a few times, was with Meredith. We loved it. When me and Darnell went it was like, something we never did before. We weren't worried. We were like, okay. Meredith wanted to make sure we packed enough clothes where we'd be warm. We'd seen it on tv so we went down the bunny slope once for practice then swoosh! It was straight down the mountain. The funny thing was, we'd go up there and we'd have like two pair of pants on and a pair of sweats and stuff, we didn't have any ski attire so we dressed in our own way. Pants falling down, we were just having a good time. It was a new experience. If we never would've met Meredith, it's not something we would have thought about. We probably never would have gone. We didn't think about going skiing one day, it's something outside of what we normally do. We loved it and not just the skiing, hanging out with Meredith and the hot cocoa and all.

***

Another memorable outing I had with Darrin and Darnell was a trip to Virginia Beach. We got up early and drove the four hours to the beach. I had my chair, towels for the boys and a cooler with cold drinks. It was a great day for the beach, sunny and hot. Neither of the boys had ever seen the ocean before, so I let them take off toward the water, racing each other to reach the small crashing waves, after warning them not to go too far out. I was content sitting in my chair under this little umbrella I had, reading a book. I glanced up often to make sure they were all right, but they both knew how to swim so I wasn't overly worried. The boys had a blast in the ocean, riding the small waves and rolling around in the breaks. Eventually I coaxed them in for something to drink and a snack, but they were anxious to return to the water. With their dark complexions I assumed they would be less likely to get sunburned than someone with fair skin. I was wrong. On the ride home, I had to listen to the moans of two young men with some pretty nasty sunburns on their skin. Lesson learned.

***

That was my first time at the beach. I'd been in the pool, of course, but it was my first experience with salt water and all that good stuff. It was my longest trip from home at the time and felt like it took forever to get down there. I can't fault Meredith for not knowing I could get sunburned, until that day I didn't know either. I was so sick! To this day I put on that sun screen.

***

At home, I would occasionally go into a big field behind a shopping center and hit golf balls. I had joined a ladies league during that time and I was really into golf for a couple of years. I could practice tee shots from the top of a small hill and then find my balls in the grass or dirt below. I'd hit a handful of balls and then take a short walk around the area collecting the balls I had hit, then do it all over again. One day Darrin was at the house with me by himself and we talked about golf. Darrin always considered himself to be a good athlete, and he did play football for Heritage High School. He made some dismissing remarks about the skills it takes to play golf and that playing golf was easy, so I bet him he couldn't hit the ball off the tee on the first swing. I told him that if I placed a golf ball on a tee at my "practice field" he'd fan the air and miss it completely. Darrin, being the cocky competitor he was bragged that he would hit the ball the very first time. I smiled to myself, knowing golf to be a finesse game and he was like a bull in a china shop. This would be fun.

We walked over to the small hill and I placed a golf ball on the tee. Darrin stepped up to the ball, holding the driver like baseball bat, prepared for a mighty swing.

"Now let's see you hit it on the first swing like you said you could," I taunted. I knew from experience that golf isn't an easy game to play, and the secret to hitting a good ball off the tee is to not try to kill it.

"Watch this," Darrin boasted as he stepped up to the ball confidently with the driver in his hand. He concentrated for a second and then took a mighty swing. Nothing but air.

I laughed out loud and he couldn't believe it. He whiffed it three or four more times and then finally connected. That ball sailed across the field farther than I had ever sent it. Darrin bragged on his drive, but did finally admit that golf was much harder than he had thought.

These were little life's lessons that created so much value in our relationship. We learned a lot from each other over the time we were together, but Darrin's biggest lesson so far was yet to come. Darrin admitted later that this particular situation caused him to be really angry with me.

I owned a Sea Doo at that time and planned to take some of the kids to Smith Mountain Lake to ride it. Darrin, Darnell, Darrin's sister, Bernice, and Curtis, a friend of Darrin's who sometimes stayed with Darrin in his basement, were all excited about the trip. Darrin, who had recently landed a job at Lynchburg General Hospital's cafeteria kitchen, was scheduled to work that day and was fit to be tied that he couldn't make the trip with us. As we were about to leave for the lake, ready to hit the road for a fun day on the water, Darrin nonchalantly joined us at the last minute. I asked him about work and he tried to sidestep a conversation. I pressed, and he admitted that he had quit so he could go to the lake with us.

"You quit your job so you could go to the lake and ride the SeaDoo?" I asked incredulously. Darrin looked down and started to explain how he didn't like the job anyway.

"Darrin, when you take a job, you take on the responsibility of being at that job when they schedule you to be there. You let your coworkers down because they had to pick up the slack for you when you left with no warning," I explained hotly. "You left your boss in the lurch too, and he was the one good enough to employ you. Anytime you leave a job you should always give two weeks notice. Plus, you don't leave a job just because you want to go to the lake and have fun."

I told him his actions were irresponsible, selfish and immature. He had never looked at it that way before, but after hearing me out he did. After seeing how upset I was, he said he was sorry and that he shouldn't have done what he did. I'm pretty sure that he thought all would work out for the day at the lake after I said what I needed to say. But it didn't. I wouldn't take him on the outing with the others. I felt bad about it, but I'm pretty sure it was a lesson he needed to learn and one I hoped that he would carry with him into adulthood. In fact, he told me years later that it was the only time he was ever really mad at me during the entire time he had known me, but he never forgot what he learned that day.

***

I was crushed. I understand it now because Meredith instilled some things in me. Because back then my boss is like 'You can't get off' and I'm like 'What? I don't need this job. I quit!' 'Then I said, 'Hey Meredith! I'm free!' Oh, no. what? But it was a good life lesson, I learned a lot. To this day I see that, but I hated it then. I was so mad at her, for like a week. And she took Darnell and Darnell kept calling me and was like 'we had the greatest time' like chew on this buddy. He rubbed it in! I was ready to fight! He called me again! My mom thought it was funny too. 'So, you quit your job, huh? Thought you was going on Smith Mountain Lake, huh? Now you're sittin' at home. Won't do that anymore will ya?' It was a tough pill to swallow. But I learned, to this day, you make a commitment to an employer. You can't just quit. You gotta give them notice.

***

A cousin of mine was on the Lynchburg police force and had participated in a raid on the home where Darnell was living with his parents and two older brothers. During the time they were inside, my cousin noticed a photo of me, Darrin and Darnell on one of their shelves. My cousin had no idea about my relationship with the boys so he assumed the worst. He related the incident to my parents and told them I should steer clear of this family. As far as I knew, they didn't have a problem with law enforcement, and I was sure Darnell didn't, and neither did Darrin. That was good enough for me. It was interesting to me that, while my cousin might have thought he had the best intentions, he assumed the worst when my relationship with the boys was actually a good thing.

Chapter 4
Separate Ways

When Darrin was a senior in high school, his mom was diagnosed with breast cancer. He told me about it, but minimized the severity, doing his usual good job of hiding his fear. Patricia went to Charlottesville for chemotherapy, and I'd take her to appointments when I could. During those rides, Patricia and I talked about a lot of things. She had met a man in prison when her other son, Will, had been locked up for selling marijuana. Fred Smith would write to her often and his letters meant the world to her. She shared some of his letters with me. They were touching and I believe they lessened her pain. She truly loved him and looked forward to him being released and being together one day. Eventually, Patricia married Fred while he was still incarcerated and before she was too ill to go through with it.

Darrin seemed to be in denial of his mother's illness. He was playing football, but eventually quit. He ran around with his friends and did what teenagers do. We still saw each other every week, but Darrin wouldn't open up to talk about how he felt and I was concerned about him. For a few hours each week, when Darrin was with me, I knew what he was into. But the rest of the time I had no idea, and it was clear Patricia wasn't in any shape to provide structure and discipline for him or Bernice.

One time when I stopped in to check on Patricia, Darrin wasn't around and Patricia didn't know where he was. I checked the basement and found Darrin there with several of his friends, smoking weed.

"I can't believe you're doing this right under your mom's nose, knowing that she's too sick to do anything about it!" I yelled. I was furious and jumped all over him. "That's totally disrespectful," I said, and then left.

As Patricia's chemo treatments continued, I lost hope that she would recover. Her health wasn't improving, but I don't think she understood that death was imminent. As she grew weaker, I drained my waterbed, packed it up and set it up for her in her bedroom, hoping the warm water circulating would help to soothe her pain. Patricia loved it and came to trust me enough to show me her breasts with lesions that looked like dark holes leaking toxic fluid. I hadn't seen anything like that before, but I knew it was bad.

A couple of things happened after that which totally changed the trajectory of Darrin's life, and mine. His mom's cancer continued to worsen, and I accepted a job promotion and moved to Alabama.

In 1995 Worrell Enterprises, the company I worked for,

flew me to Baldwin County, Alabama over the July 4th weekend. I was supposed to look around and decide if I wanted to live there, and more importantly if I would want the job they were offering. Worrell Enterprises owned a group of six community newspapers near the Gulf of Mexico called Gulf Coast Newspapers. If I agreed to go there, I would publish community newspapers in Daphne, Fairhope, Gulf Shores, Loxley, Robertsdale, Foley and Bay Minette.

My first night there, I learned about July 4th fireworks being held at the Fairhope pier. Throngs of locals were down at the waterfront waiting for the fireworks to begin. I made my way to the edge of the water and hung my feet over one of the wooden pilings. As I sat there watching the display, a calm came over me, a sense of peace that I will never forget. I was exactly where I should be, as though God had opened this door for me and was with me. I didn't know a soul at that busy marina, but I could feel a sense of love from all of them.

During my visit, I drove by a house that I really liked from the outside. The Realtor who had the listing for that home happened to live across the street from the property. Tom, her husband, was working in their yard. I stopped and expressed my interest in the home to Tom. He told me his wife, Lynne, was at home and could show me the listing right away. Lynne took me inside and I immediately fell in love with it. I returned to Lynchburg on Sunday night and accepted the job Monday morning. A friend of mine, Ann Marie Myers, called that day to see if I wanted to play golf and I told her I couldn't, that I was moving to Alabama and had tons of stuff to do. Anne Marie had been in my house before and told me she and her husband, Steve, would like to come over and see my house. They made an offer on my home that evening which I accepted. Some things are meant to happen. Within three days, I had traveled to Alabama, put an offer on a home, sold my home and accepted a new job.

I talked to Darrin about my plans. I knew he would be sad, but I reassured him that even though we'd be far apart, I loved him and would be just a phone call away. Darrin and Darnell were becoming men and no longer had the same interests or needs that they had as kids. The BBBS program has an age out limit of 17 years old, and Darrin was at that pivotal juncture. I knew that with his mother so sick, it would be rough, but I also knew everybody has to handle these hardships in their own way. I did have reservations about Darrin and Bernice living with a bedridden mother, but Patricia's sister, Nancy, was only an hour away and could check on things and handle any emergencies. I knew that the bond between Darrin and me wouldn't be broken if I moved away; it would stretch, and that stretching would be good for both of our lives.

***

When Meredith went to Alabama, at that time, I was coming to terms with, I think, our relationship coming to an end, or not coming to an end, but once she moved and I was getting older, I knew things were changing and I kinda accepted it. We weren't hanging out once a week or whatever. Once she moved to Alabama, it was understood. I knew it couldn't last the same way forever. By that time I was seventeen or eighteen. I don't want to say I was in a fog, it was just my attitude. I wasn't focused on anything. My mom was sick, I was hanging out with people, smoking weed. We still talked then but never in detail, not, like my feelings. I never told her, like, I was afraid my mom was going to die or this or that, never in detail. But I didn't talk to anybody about that. I don't talk to a lot of people like that. Conversation like, when you talk about feelings, I've never been a feelings person, "I feel this" or "I feel that", "I feel afraid" "I feel scared". I didn't grow up in a household like that so it's not something normal to me, I guess. To this day I don't. And I'll get that from some people. "You'll tell me just enough to be good, but not enough in detail about what's going on in your head. I can never get inside!"

Within a week, I was packed up and on my way to a new life in Alabama. I was 35, single, and looking for a change. I had been working at the local newspaper for fourteen years and had dated some, including Rick. That relationship had ended a few years ago and there were no new relationships on the horizon. A change of scenery was just what I needed.

I moved into the new house in Daphne, Alabama and my Realtor, Lynne, and her husband, Tom, began a friendship with me that quickly grew. Before long, I became extended family. They were laid back and fun and had two teenage daughters, Sarah and Lisa, who were the same way. Lynne was a nice mix of mom, sister and friend to me. She was a great cook and invited me across the street for laughter-filled meals often. We loved to go shopping together, with Lynn showing me places that I had no idea existed. Sometimes the three of us would go out for dinner and drinks. Without a doubt, they made my move from Virginia to Alabama a pleasure. I was never lonely or apprehensive. I fit right in.

My new house was awesome. It was all on one level, with grey cedar siding and a large carport area. It was located on the 13th hole of the community golf course and the backyard was shaded by tall pines and landscaped with rhododendrons, azaleas and other low growing bushes. The coolest part of my front yard was the two tall palm trees. They were healthy and full and seemed so exotic to this Virginian.

The inside of the house was nice as well. It had a large kitchen which was destined to remain largely unused, a spacious living room with a rock fireplace and three bedrooms. It also featured a central vacuum system, a novelty I totally appreciated the first time I used it. I felt capable, independent and confident the move to Alabama was going to be good for me in the long run.

I started work almost immediately, assuming responsibility for the revenue and operations of six small newspapers and managing 72 employees. Gulf Coast Newspapers had been publishing these local papers there for many years, three of them for more than a century. The county was growing at a fast pace and many of my employees had been in their jobs for years and knew their work well, making my job pretty easy. While I developed ideas over a short time and implemented some, there was no reason to make sweeping changes. The "if it ain't broke, don't try to fix it" concept applied here.

Large pecan groves graced the spaces between many of the small towns like Loxley, Summerdale and Foley. From Gulf Shores all the way up to Perdido Key in Escambia County the beaches were sugar-white and filled with tourists. Bars and restaurants dotted the landscape, but there were not as many high-rise hotels or condos back then. It was still a simple time really; the beaches and surrounding areas were a secret that Alabama residents kept well. Most of my free time was spent riding my Sea Doo, laying out on the beach, eating fresh seafood, and drinking nice cold beer.

One of my favorite places to go was the Florabama, a legendary bar situated directly on the Florida-Alabama line. It looked like a beach shack that kept being added onto over time. The actual workmanship was good, but it was disguised to look like a giant, sprawling mess. It was a classic dive bar with all kinds of sayings, drawings and signatures on the walls, contributions from patrons over the years. The different sections featured areas for live music and many different bars to serve the consistently huge crowds, both inside and out. The walls were decorated with photos, lights, beads, and even the life-sized head of a wild boar over the bar which sported several lacy bras hanging from it. Another area had a pool table that was almost always being played by someone for pocket change. The theme was rustic, dilapidated and generally disreputable. The Florabama also held fundraising events to benefit non-profit organizations such as the mullet toss, a competition where participants would throw dead fish as far as they could to determine the winners. I'm pretty sure the owners were strong marketers, because they had no trouble attracting customers, day or night. I was, and still am, a big fan of the Florabama.

I was in a good place in my life when I lived in Alabama and I did not want it to end. But it did.

After a year in paradise, my boss, Benny Jones, informed me that he was going to buy the newspapers and wanted to run them himself. Benny offered me a year's salary if I would sign a non-compete agreement, and he would even rent my house from me when I left. I had just begun to grow my wings and was not happy about the situation, but there was nothing I could do, so I accepted his offer reluctantly. I soon found myself saying goodbye to my new friends and employees, packing up and heading back to Lynchburg.

Chapter 5
Transitions

Thankfully, The News & Advance hired me again to handle some special publications. I found a small house to rent belonging to my old neighbors who used to live across the street from me. They owned a body shop conveniently located almost directly across from the newspaper and my new home was tucked behind it. After a few weeks in town, I realized I had just been living in Lynchburg for too long and at that newspaper for too many years to suit me. I couldn't shake the disappointment of feeling like I'd taken a giant step backwards, and I kept my eyes open for new opportunities.

Finding myself somewhat at loose ends, I decided to use my spare time wisely on some small projects, like building an air-conditioned doghouse for my bulldog, Roscoe. Because of his breed he couldn't be left outside in hot weather for very long, and there were times I couldn't get home to let him out for hours. I built it, and it worked, and he loved it, but my friends and family and I had a lot of laughs over it. It looked okay, but I was no Bob Vila, and the idea of how pampering this was for that silly old bulldog was just too amusing.

The air conditioned dog house I built for Roscoe.

The best part about coming home was being able to see and talk to Darrin regularly. Now that I was back in Lynchburg, we fell right back into our old routine and saw each other weekly, which was good for us both.

Within four months of returning to Lynchburg, a newspaper head-hunter contacted me and recommended me for a position at The Daily Times in Salisbury, Maryland. The position was for Advertising Director, something I had done before. It was in a market smaller than Lynchburg, but I didn't care as long as it offered a new challenge in a new environment. The job included a $5,000 signing bonus and a good salary as well. I interviewed for the position and was hired. The publisher who hired me, Jane Reid, looked to be in her late fifties and had a wealth of newspaper experience. She was a likable person and I thought we would work well together.

I soon found myself living in a three-level condo in Salisbury located on the Wicomico River, a perfect arrangement for docking and riding my Sea Doo. The size of the condo was more than I needed unless I had company. Not too long after I moved there, Darrin, Darnell, Bernice and Curtis, a long time friend, came up for a visit. We took the Sea Doo out on the brackish river, which wasn't clean and clear like the lake we had been used to. They didn't like it as much, but we still had a great time. They spent the night and went home to Lynchburg the next day. It sure was good to have so many happy young people to spend time with.

My work at the newspaper was stressful because it wasn't generating the revenue upper management expected, and much of that pressure fell on me. When they hired me, I was aware that the publisher expected high revenue growth. After all, that's a big part of the equation for a newspaper's profitability. What I didn't know was how big a gap existed between where they were and where they wanted to be. I found process issues and poor performance in every department. It was not a good situation, and all I could do was chip away at the problems within my own department and work with others to create new ideas for generating more sales. I felt comfortable with Jane, who seemed to be aware that the newspaper had been heading down the wrong road for years. She was patient as we worked together to figure out ways to improve our revenue numbers.

Salisbury was not the sort of city that boasted a big nightlife like the larger beach area of Ocean City, Maryland. It was only a short distance away, but going to the beach by myself wasn't much fun. I called Gaither Perry, a close friend who published The Suffolk News Herald at the time. Gaither and I had been friends for years, and I had learned a lot about the business from him. In fact, he had been up for the same publisher's position in Alabama and there were no hard feelings when they had passed him over for me.

One night, in April 1996, the two of us agreed to meet for dinner on the Eastern Shore. We picked Wachapreague, a small fishing village, for our meeting, close to a mid-point for our travels. It was a chilly Saturday evening when I drove down to the tiny little town, found the Island House Restaurant, and parked my car in the crowded lot. I hurried inside to warm up and found a spot at the busy bar. I was blowing into my hands trying to warm them and figure out what to order while I waited for Gaither. A big guy sitting next to me at the bar noticed and suggested I get an Irish coffee or something to warm me up.

"Good idea!" I ordered my favorite: coffee and Kahlua.

The big guy introduced himself as Joe Collins, and we chatted easily as I sipped my drink.

He was in the Navy, based out of Norfolk it turned out, not a Wachapreague resident.

"My brother owns a house in Quinby, down the road," he said. "I like to drive up occasionally and look after the place and maybe go fishing."

The longer we visited, the more I liked Joe. He seemed very smart and had a tremendous sense of humor. He also seemed genuine and, best of all, I could tell he liked talking with me, too.

I started to get a little worried about Gaither since he was about an hour overdue. As I was trying to figure out what to do, Gaither popped in the door complaining of my bad directions and how he had gotten all turned around when trying to find me. Joe and I laughed in relief and Gaither ordered a drink while I introduced him to Joe. Once Gaither and I decided we were hungry, we got a table and I invited Joe to join us.

From that day forward, I was no longer lonely in Salisbury. Because of his Navy work, Joe was either in Norfolk or out to sea most of the time, but he wrote the best letters. I think it was through his letter writing skills that I fell in love with him. It turned out to be a great way to get to know each other without constantly being distracted by hormones. When Joe could, he drove up to Salisbury to see me or I'd visit him in Norfolk. Sometimes we would meet at his brother's place in Quinby to spend time together. It's funny how things work out in life. With all the intimacy difficulties I had in the past, baggage from my young life, I rarely had any anxiety about being with Joe. It felt right. We would take walks, watch television or maybe go out for a bite to eat, and I was comfortable. Occasionally I would feel a little unsettled, but Joe had a way of minimizing it. He was warm, attentive and I could tell how he felt about me. We talked and laughed, and I was glad to have him in my life.

My love life was heating up, but things at work were taking a turn for the worse. The Daily Times was owned by Thomson Newspapers, and they were determined to increase profitability with their newspapers. Many higher ups were getting the chop, and I was really upset when they replaced Jane Reid as publisher with Bob Brown, who didn't have a kind disposition. Bob was bent on axing current department heads to move in his own people. One evening around 6:00, Bob suddenly called me into his office and fired me. He gave no reason and I didn't ask. I knew I'd done a good job but nothing I could say was going to change the outcome. I cleaned out my desk and went home. The next day I tried to reach Joe with no luck. I left him a message: "Call me back. I've been fired!"

While I'd been gone, Darrin's mom's health continued to deteriorate, and she was admitted to Virginia Baptist Hospital. I went to visit Patricia there and she had lost so much weight that she didn't even resemble the woman I had first met eight years ago. Darrin wasn't with his mother and I wondered if his way of coping with the coming loss was to stay away and remain in denial. I reached out to him and I told him if he had anything to say to his mom that this was the time, because she wouldn't be with us much longer. She had been his mom, his world. He would never have another chance to thank her and tell her goodbye. We arranged to meet on the sidewalk in front of the hospital, where we hugged. This would be the last time Darrin ever saw his mother alive.

Patricia passed away on September 14, 1996. She was only 39 years old, and Darrin was an orphan at the age of 18.

They held a memorial service for Patricia Banner at Trinity United Methodist Church in Lynchburg. I remember walking in and noticing that I was the only white person there. I wasn't uncomfortable because everybody I interacted with was warm and embracing. That's how it always should be, and that's how it was. Patricia was buried in Forest Hill Burial Park on Lakeside Drive in Lynchburg. All her children were there, and some relatives that I had met before. Patricia's husband, Fred, wore an orange jumpsuit and handcuffs, accompanied by a prison guard. I had not met him before, but felt I knew him through his letters Patricia shared with me. She had always spoken so well of him.

***

While I was in high school my mom was sick. I wasn't thinking about that or this. She's gonna be all right. She's not that sick, she's gonna make it through this, she's not gonna die. I didn't want to know how bad it was. She never really told me. Nobody told me your mom's not gonna make it. I remember one of the last conversations we had was when I was with her at the hospital, a few days before she died. It was just me and her. She was crying and I think she felt bad cause she knew she wasn't going to be there, and she was apologizing and saying she's sorry and all that so from that point I realized it may be more than what I had been thinking.

A few days later, I was at a football game and my cousin was there. His mom called him to say that my mom had passed. He told me and I rode to the hospital.

It never dawned on me that she was that sick. I always thought she was going to beat it. She'd been strong her whole life, like Superman. I regret that part, cause it was time we could have talked and I could have been with her. I knew the whole time she was on medicine and she was going to chemotherapy and she would go into remission. I didn't understand any of it, and maybe I was in denial. After my mom died in September, we went to Salisbury for a week. Me, Bernice and Curt. School had started, so we took time off from school.

Nowadays when I think about my mom, it is more than just sadness. I'm at a point in my life when I want to know stuff like family history, illness, things I don't know. Issues I could talk to her about or even memories where we could say, "Remember when this happened?" There's so much I don't know.

I never had an adult talk with her. I had just turned 18 when she died, but she was sick when I was 16, 17. I can't have conversations with her now. Or or even just bring up stuff like, "You know when this happened when we were younger?" I realized that she and my sister had different conversations than my brother and I had with her. Some of that made me jealous, but she's a girl, and she gets different stuff. Bernice would mention something and I'm like, "I didn't' know that!" I wish she had talked to me about that. But mom always had a saying, she said she had no favorites, even though I knew I was her favorite. But I thought that was cool that she talked to Bernice like that.

We have a lot of family members and friends who are nurses and mom was a nurse. I asked Bernice, "Why didn't you become a nurse?" and she said, "Momma told me never become a nurse.

Told me you don't want this job, don't do this," and so she shied away from it. Small things like that I missed. I am sure there are other conversations we would have had. I miss that the most. What was it like when she was a teenager? Or even when she met my dad? I mean, my dad was a smooth kinda guy and she was this little country girl who got swept up in his charm. And I think maybe I'm kinda like that. So just another thing I'd talk to her about. I'd hear from a lot of relatives and my mom how I acted like and did certain things like my dad. And my dad. I know less about him than anybody.

My mom was sweet, always very positive and very sweet and smiled, always had a smile on her face. The sweetest lady. Even with a lot going on, you wouldn't know. I guess she internalized things too. You wouldn't know unless she told you. You wouldn't read it on her face, but you might catch her alone crying or something like that. I am at an age now that she never made it to. I think about that.

Darrin as a teenager.

So, I was unemployed then and living in Fruitland, just outside of Salisbury, where I found an older home for less rent. Many of those first days after I was fired were spent on the roof. I would climb out my bedroom window, throw a beach towel down to lie on and soak in the sun. For some reason, I wasn't as worried as I should have been about finding another job. Maybe it was because because Joe was present in my life and came to visit often, spending time with me and listening to my work woes. His strong support kept my fears at bay.

I soon decided to get serious about my future and contacted my old boss, Benny Jones, who was still living in my house in Daphne, Alabama. He wanted me to return to Alabama to work for him at Gulf Coast Newspapers on specialty products. He also told me he would move out of my house so I could move in. I really loved Alabama but I agonized over the decision on whether to move or not. I had only been dating Joe for a short while then and I liked where things seemed to be going. I didn't want to move that far away from him, yet it was too soon for either of us to make a commitment. I finally came to the conclusion that if we were meant to be, time and distance would not change that.

My return to Alabama was the stuff of classic old comedies. I had an ancient truck, a Jeep Comanche that I modified for the trip. I added makeshift railings on the sides and two by fours and other stuff until it brought to mind Jed Clampett's truck on the Beverly Hillbillies. Our plan was that I would drive the Jeep and Joe would follow in a Ryder truck, towing my Honda Accord.

I planned to travel with my two dogs in the back of the truck with their beds, so we had to make sure it was escape-proof. Little Snow, my beautiful, white, longhaired cat, would ride up front with me. To fully appreciate this story, you have to know more about my dogs. Roscoe was a big-footed, slobbery bulldog with awesome brindle markings who I'd bought from a breeder when he was a year old. He had great bloodlines, but he'd grown so large that the breeder couldn't show him. Roscoe was a giant sweetheart and loved to chill. As a potential show dog and stud, he wasn't yet neutered, and he was pretty insistent about checking the situation out if he sensed a female might be willing. Kayla, my light brown Chocolate lab, was the total opposite of Roscoe. She was as manic as Roscoe was laid back, a high-energy dog who seemed happiest when she was running somewhere. It didn't matter where. I suspected it would be a challenge to contain Kayla on this trip.

It's just under 800 miles from Lynchburg to Daphne, Alabama. We had planned to travel until we got tired and then find a pet-friendly place to spend the night, finishing the trip the next day. Well, the plan was good, but the execution was anything but. We drove quite a ways and then made a stop for gas. Little Snow decided she had had enough of being cooped up in the front seat with me and squeezed out of a partially open window, making a break for the woods behind the gas station. I don't know how much time we spent looking frantically for her, but there was no way I was going to leave without her. My baby was lost, and I was so afraid I wouldn't find her, or someone would pick her up. Finally, Little Snow came strolling out of the trees and declared herself ready to get back in the truck. She acted, as cats do, as if she'd done nothing wrong and couldn't see what all the fuss was about.

At one point in our journey, the Jeep Cherokee (a.k.a. Clampett's truck) truck bed contraption started coming apart and it began to rain. Stuff moved around in the bed of the truck and the dogs were getting spooked and wet. My "expert" workmanship was not holding up under 70 mph road conditions. We finally accepted that we couldn't keep them back there safely anymore and decided to put them in the cab of the Ryder truck with Joe. That worked well for a short while until Mother Nature intervened and Roscoe got a whiff of Kayla starting to come into heat. Who knew? I hadn't owned her very long, and with getting ready to move, I hadn't had time to even think about her going into season, much less having her spayed. Poor Joe had to drive with one arm and wrestle persistent Roscoe and poor Kayla apart with the other for the remainder of the trip. Not to mention hold them both in his lap and comfort them every time the truck would backfire. I'm surprised Joe didn't end our relationship then and there.

Things didn't get much better when we arrived in Daphne. I had gotten migraine headaches off and on throughout my life but the one that came on in Alabama was the mother of them all. The pain was so bad that I was totally incapacitated. Joe unloaded a mattress as soon as he could and got me situated while I laid on the mattress like a corpse. Then, he proceeded to unload the animals, secure them, and unload everything I owned from the Clampett truck, the Ryder and my Accord. I felt terrible about it, but there was nothing I could do. Joe got everything inside the house and even started putting some of the most necessary items in their place. I don't know too many people that would hold up under those circumstances - physically, mentally or emotionally. But my man did, and when night came upon us and the animals were fed, we all slept soundly.

The next day, I felt better and was able to start working inside the house. Tom and Lynne came over to see us and were glad I was back. They had not met Joe before, but I could tell they immediately liked him. Joe turned in the Ryder truck and we spent the next couple of days working around the house, enjoying cold beer, and eating at a couple of the local restaurants.

There were lots of great bars and restaurants that I wanted to share with Joe in Gulf Shores, but this time we stayed close to home around Daphne and Fairhope. One of the coolest bars in this area was called Judge Roy Beans, and was owned by well-known musician Jimmy Buffet. It was an outdoor venue complete with dirt floors and a goat that made itself right at home. It was always packed with locals and tourists alike in its day. Joe and I made a stop there, followed by Manci's Antique Bar in Daphne, a small stand-alone building that was completely covered in antiques on the walls, ceilings, shelves and everywhere you could think of. It was dark inside Manci's, with a bar to the right, some seating and a few pool tables to the left. The women's restroom was its most famous attraction. Directly in front of the bar's only stall is a wooden statue of a man, naked except for a modest fig leaf on a hinge. If a lady succumbed to temptation and lifted the fig leaf to take a peek at the statue's anatomy, a loud alarm bell would go off in the bar, letting everyone in the bar know that she looked. This happened to me once, but of course never again. I got a kick out of bringing in other unsuspecting friends whose curiosity inevitably got the best of them, too.

That first weekend in Alabama with Joe, we had a wild experience on my Sea Doo. We hopped on and took it down toward Orange Beach, stopping for a break and a beer at Tacky Jack's, one of my favorite stops when I'm on the water. We headed for the Intracoastal Waterway which begins near Ono Island. I'd never taken the Sea Doo there before, but we both thought it would be a nice ride. We were doubling with Joe driving and me with my arms wrapped tight around his waist when two huge boats passed by going in different direction, both moving fast. I'm not sure what they were, fishing boats or cruisers, I just know they each generated giant wakes, and we were caught in the middle of a perfect storm. Our little Sea Doo shot up in the air, riding the top of a giant water spout, and then we plummeted straight down fast and smacked the water. Joe's chin hit the handle bars hard and I fell off, scraping my thigh down the side of the Jet Ski as I hit the water. Stunned, we assessed the damage, which turned out to be minimal. I'm thankful we weren't killed. We were unaware of how powerful those wakes could be.

Joe could only stay for a few days before he had to get back to Norfolk. The original plan was for him to catch a military flight to the base because it would be free. Unfortunately, there were no military flights during the right time period, so we bought him a one-way ticket at the Mobile Regional Airport. We both cried when it was time for him to leave. I knew then that it was foolish for me to take that job in Alabama and that my second time there would be shorter than my first. There were too many miles between Alabama and Virginia.

I went to work for Benny right away. He wanted me to create a print product reaching the homes in a large Daphne neighborhood called Lake Forest. It happened to be where I lived, so I understood the demographics and why businesses would want to reach this market. It wasn't a wealthy, gated community but it was upper middle class and significant in size. Denny's hope was to gain some market share from Mobile, just a short drive across Mobile Bay. On paper this made a lot of sense, but it was a lot more difficult to turn the concept into reality.

During this time I kept in touch with Darrin by phone. It was hard to know how he was really doing because I knew him well enough to know that he wouldn't voluntarily tell me anything bad. I was having a good time in Alabama and wanted him to find his way as an independent young man. In retrospect I could have kept in touch a little closer during that time, but I didn't foresee anything bad coming around the bend. I expected too much from Darrin and didn't fully understand how his losses were impacting him emotionally. What happened next hit me by surprise, like a head-on collision between a Mack truck and a Volkswagen.

Chapter 6
Sidelined

I'd just turned 18. My birthday was in July, and my mom passed in September. I was a senior. She passed away the beginning of my senior year. When she passed, Meredith came, then we spent a week in Maryland to ease our minds, then it was back to reality. I went back to school, and all the people in my classes and the football team was very supportive. They had shown up at the funeral.

Everybody was supportive but it changed, because Bernice and I were staying at the house. We still got social security checks from my father, me and Bernice. Will too, but once you turn 18 they stop. So, we used some of that and tried to pay the bills, and the mortgage on the house. I was going to school, and still played football.

Life had changed because I was my own adult. I could go to school and I could leave whenever I wanted because I was my own guardian. I don't feel like being here, I can leave. Mostly I didn't cause football kept me there. If I wanted to play football

I had to go to school. I had to maintain my grades and I was still kind of doing that, but that was the only incentive. Bernice and I took care of each other. By that time, I went to school, but I had friends coming over to the house and we'd drink or smoke or whatever. Bernice wanted to hang out too, but I made sure Bernice still went to school and didn't stay up too late.

Darrin as a football player for Heritage High School.

In November, we had maybe one more football game left, and that's when I got the news that my grandpa had had a stroke. I was on the phone all night with Nancy. We had a football game that night. It was a Friday night and I got the news that night, and we had practice on Saturday. So, even though I was up all night talking to Nancy, I still went to practice that Saturday. Coach didn't want you coming in late, and I came in late. And you got a penalty to pay for that. You had to run hills or whatever after practice. But I explained to him my situation. On top of my mom dying just a couple of months ago, my grandfather just had a massive stroke. I don't know if he is going to die, and he is in the hospital on life support. I'd been up all night, but I'm here and practicing, and he was like, "I understand that."

At the end of practice he's calling out the names of everybody that came to practice late and he called my name out and said, "King, get over here." So, I get over there and he is like, "You all are running these hills." And I'm running the hills then I'm like, at this time, you know what? "Fuck this shit.' I got all this shit to deal with. Ya'll are lucky I came to practice at all. So, I felt like I'd explained it. I shouldn't have to do this. I dropped my stuff and I quit. I didn't want to quit. But, all my life, when I quit, people always came to me with "we want you back, don't do that." You know, they talk to you and all that. That's all I wanted from the coach, but I never got that. He was stubborn. I was stubborn. We only had one game left, you know. I realized I had a couple of offers from schools. Not big schools but like Tusculum and Elon College, to play football. But the coach never said anything about them, never cultivated it or anything. So, I didn't have a lot of love for him. After I quit football, maybe a couple of weeks later, I dropped out of school.

I wasn't really doing anything but bills still had to be paid and I didn't have a job. I sold a little weed every once in a while.

I smoked a little weed. I hung out. That is when Bernice tried hanging out with me some at the house but I was like, you got to go to sleep at 10 or 11 o'clock, you got school tomorrow. And at the time she hated me for that. "You're not my mom. You can't do this." To the point where, after a certain amount time she said "I'm going to go live with Nancy, our Aunt." Two or three weeks later she came back. She thought I was strict but Nancy was even stricter, kind of like mom. We actually needed that, but at that time Bernice was forming her own mind frame and she was tough already. She didn't listen to a lot of people. My mom, she would listen to. Anybody else wasn't on their level. I always looked out for her, even though I dropped out my mom didn't want her to drop out, so I tried to make sure she went to school and she was good.

***

One day, upon arriving home, I discovered a letter from Jim Brent in my mailbox. Jim and I had worked together at the Lynchburg newspaper for the fourteen years I was there, but I had known him even longer than that. Jim was known around town for his long career in sales at The News & Advance. To me, he was a really nice guy who would lend me his rusty old truck whenever I needed to haul something. If you needed help with almost anything, Jim would almost always volunteer. He was a giver in every sense of the word.

When I opened his letter, out fell a clipping of a newspaper article with a Post-it attached that read, "Isn't this your Darrin?" The headline told the story of two boys stealing some items from a woman and her son at gunpoint. The robbery occurred in Lynchburg on August 8, 1997, and one of the robbers named was Darrin King. I read it in disbelief. Darrin, while mischievous, had never shown any sign of doing anything remotely like that before. Where in the world did he get a gun? Was it loaded? Who was the young fellow with him? I was going to have to do some research to answer my questions, but first I needed to call Joe and tell him.

Darrin was locked up, so I knew I would have to be patient before I could talk to him face to face. The only explanation I could guess for this behavior was the loss of his mother. He was very close to her and always spoke highly of her. In addition, my move to Alabama removed one of his most constant sources of support.

At the same time, Joe and I had already been making plans for me to move closer to him. The job I had was okay, but not really what I wanted to be doing. Being back in Alabama was great, but no longer awesome since Joe was so far away. I had been pursuing at job at The Virginian-Pilot in Norfolk, and hoped it would be a challenging newspaper position where I could achieve promotions over the years ahead. Being back in Virginia would also put me closer to Darrin. I had no idea what the outcome of his upcoming trial would be, but I did know that holding a loaded gun during a robbery was going to be a significant problem for him.

As it turned out, I was offered a sales position at The Virginian-Pilot. I was a little disappointed since I had been a publisher and had held management positions in the past with an excellent track record. After I had been there long enough, I realized that their culture valued some people differently than others. But at the time, I took the job and it paid fairly well. I was happy to be back with Joe and closer to my parents, and I could get back into Darrin's life again. Given what I had recently learned about the trouble he'd gotten himself into, I planned to make him a priority. If he really did commit that crime, I knew he would have to do some time. That really upset me, because I had heard enough about prisons to know I didn't want Darrin to be there.

So, four months after he brought me to Alabama, Joe travelled back there to help me move to Virginia. This time, fortunately, I didn't have a migraine, so I was a lot more help. Sadly, I had to find a home for my chocolate lab, Kayla, since we wouldn't have anywhere for her to run when we returned. I was grateful to find someone who loved her and owned lots of land where she could run free and live her best life. It really saddened me to leave her behind, but I still had my couch potato, Roscoe.

***

It was a chain of events. My mom, my grandpa, I quit football, I dropped out of school. I was not working at the time. I was hanging out, making a little money selling weed to my friends and whatever, nothing serious. At the same time, Curt and Geoff basically lived with me, my two best friends forever. They were helping out too, and another guy Derrick, he was one of my closest friends. Me and Derrick were hanging out. We had been friends since elementary school like Curt. So, me and

Derrick are hanging out and he's not going to school and we're like, we need some money, we're not working. I still don't know how the concept of robbing somebody came up. We never were around people like that, no stealing, no gunplay or nothing like that. But I had access to it, I was hanging in the streets more, being around more people like that and you're selling weed and you get in different beefs, arguments and stuff. I had a few issues like that and I wanted to be ready. That night, we drove around, low on money, and I might have gotten high earlier. I had a gun from an earlier incident with some guy. This guy was like, "I'm gonna get my gun," so eventually I got a gun in case I was out and about again I, wouldn't be without one.

So, a stupid thing, stupid and reckless at the time, all I'm thinking about is basically keeping the house so Bernice can stay in school. I wasn't thinking about getting in trouble or the law or anything. I just didn't care, I was invincible. You can't touch me. Me and Derrick were riding around, and it's like, we got this gun, we need some money, we're gonna jack somebody. And we thought that, being we're in the hood, maybe we can catch somebody, a hustler, somebody slipping, somebody that's in the hood dicking around. So, we're driving around and it was through chance we saw this guy in a truck sitting out. So, we drive by him and eventually we park the car, jump out, me and Derrick. All I got on is a shirt and I kind of got it draped over my hand. We see the guy and I go up to him. He's in his car, the windows down, I go up I'm like "Just give me all your money" and he was saying something like "I don't got anything on me. I'm here to pick up my mom." I'm like, "Give me your wallet."

At that same time, his grandmother walks up behind me,

coming out of the house, so I turned around. I still got the gun, I'm shaking and she's shaking, and she's like, "I don't have any money." So, I said, "Let's get out of here." She turned around and runs back in the house. I told the guy to give me his wallet, and we took off, running up the street, jump back in the car, and we take off.

The sad thing about it, if we was thinking it out or would have been career criminals or something. We left and were still driving around, not a care in the world, instead of going home. It was late at night. We could have just gone home. In a way, I kind of see it as fate or destiny. It was good cause if we wouldn't have got caught, we might have done worse. Something else could have happened.

We were driving up Fort Avenue in Lynchburg and a cop passed us and turned around and got behind us. The guy had already reported us. He got a visual of the car, some description. We're not thinking that, the cop has turned around and he's behind us and now he's got the lights on. That was maybe 20 to 30 minutes after it happened. It was a random guy we robbed and we were just riding around after for the hell of it, but there's a possibility that if we hadn't got stopped, we would have done it again. There was like eight dollars or so in his wallet. It wasn't a lot. It definitely wasn't worth it, 8 years of your life!

They took us to the jail, and they're talking to us. The officer is like, "You know, we already know you all did it. You may as well go ahead and confess." But I had seen too many cop shows, so I'm like, "I don't know what you're talking about. We didn't do anything. You just pulled us over." It was Derrick's car and *they found the gun under the passenger seat and I was driving the car, so of course they offered me a deal. They're like, "If you go ahead and tell us that your friend is the one who did it, we'll offer you three months boot camp." I'm thinking, I'm not gonna say that cause that didn't happen. I'm still thinking, I'm not gonna plead guilty to anything cause we can defeat this in court. When they first pulled us over, they brought the guy out there, and he said, "I think that's the guy and pointed at Derrick," and later he said, "I think it was the other guy." So, he didn't know who it was. He was scared shitless. So, I could've put it on him, but it turned out they gave Derrick the same deal, and he got three months boot camp.*

They didn't give me a lawyer right away and I didn't ask for one. They put me in a little annex first, then in a cold cell, by myself, and I was thinking, "What the hell did I get myself into?" As soon as they closed the gates I am ready to tear up and keep thinking "What the fuck did I get myself into? What the fuck did I just do?" I had no idea that it carried, like, 8 years, no idea. In my mind I knew I wasn't gonna hurt the guy. I got four charges. I got a robbery, attempted robbery, possession of a firearm, and commission of a felony. They said when I turned around and pointed the gun at her and she said "I don't have any money," that was attempted robbery. And they gave me the gun charge for that and for pointing it at him. The gun charge carries mandatory time. Three years for the first time and five years for the second time. So, that's two gun charges right there. I was there for a day. You don't have a clock, the light stays on 24/7, you don't know what time of day it is, no windows or nothing, and nobody to communicate with. You get a phone call.

I called Bernice and let her know what was going on. Then they shipped me across the street to the big jail.

I didn't talk to Meredith through all of this. I didn't want to tell her. I didn't want her to know I was going through this, or whatever. I still had hopes that maybe I wouldn't go to prison. Same denial that I had with my mom. My lawyer told me I could get a minimum of eight years and I thought, "Nah." I was like, the guy didn't know who did it so I think we have a good case. Later, he told me my co-defendant might testify against me, because they offered him the same deal they had offered me. I'm like, he wouldn't do that. I saw him and asked, "They said you're gonna testify against me?" And he said "No, no!" But he did. He sat there in court and set me up and ratted me out.

***

I returned to Virginia in time to attend Darrin's sentencing in Lynchburg. He was sentenced to eight years for two counts of robbery, both with a loaded gun. His take was just only eight dollars and a credit card. I was blown away. I knew it was his actions that determined his sentencing, not what he lifted, but I still had no idea he would get that much time. We heard later that the other boy who was there during the crime rolled over on Darrin in exchange for receiving no prison time. My heart ached for Darrin as Joe and I waited outside the courthouse with the hopes of speaking to Darrin as they moved him from the courtroom to the waiting van. He shuffled along wearing an orange jumpsuit and shackles, and it broke my heart. I tried to talk to him, tears running down my face.

"Can I please give Darrin a hug?" I said to the guard.

"I'm sorry ma'am. You are not allowed to come close," the guard replied.

"Please let me talk to him and give him a hug," I begged repeatedly, face awash in tears.

The guard finally relented and showed some compassion. I hugged him briefly and talked to him as he continued to move Darrin along to the transfer vehicle. Darrin looked distressed at seeing me like that. He tried for a stiff upper lip, but I could see past it. Those were our last moments before they whisked Darrin away in a van and he was gone.

**

Tough. Emotional. It was tough because I knew I'd disappointed her. I felt like I let her down. And I hate to see her cry. I see her cry and it makes me emotional. And I let her down on top of that plus I got the weight of this eight years on me. So, all of this and seeing her was a lot. And then you get back and you can't show these emotions, no crying, no teary eyed. I stayed in the cell the rest of the day. With my handling emotions and processing everything, it wouldn't have been good for me to be around people, could wind up in a fight or anything could happen. So, I stayed in my cell for a couple of days and processed everything and tried to deal with everything.

**

After some time in the Lynchburg city jail, they moved Darrin to Deep Meadows Correctional Center in State Farm, Virginia, where I received my introduction to prisons and all of their many rules. Deep Meadows is a medium security prison, a good thing, but I knew Darrin's future really depended on the inmates inside and the Correctional

Officers (COs) there. One unhappy inmate with a shank or a CO who has it in for you, and the course of events could change in a minute. In prison, inmates are not allowed to handle cash, so Joe and I had to work within the system to give Darrin anything. We could add money to his commissary account so he could obtain simple needs like snacks or sodas or toiletries, and Joe looked into getting him a couple of newspaper subscriptions so he could keep up with major events in the outside world.

***

I think I was in jail a week, week and a half, then I got out on bond. Curtis had a family that dealt with bonds and things like that, so I think that guy put his house up and I had to give him a thousand dollars, and he bonded me out, and I was out until the trial. Once I got out, I got a job at Sam's Club. My lawyer, public defender, was telling me you gotta get a job, you gotta do this, you gotta do that. He told me they would look favorable on me if I got a job and started working, so I started working. It was a tire technician job. I wish I would have found that before.

I don't remember how long I was out before I went to trial. It was months, but when I went to trial they found me guilty and immediately locked me up again. Between the time I got locked up and my sentencing and the time I went to prison it was all kind of like a blur. It was like six months, I was in the jail, guilty, and I am ready to be sentenced. I want them to go ahead and sentence me. From the time I got my sentence to the time I went to prison was like eight months and I am going crazy. I already know I had my time and I am ready to go. I'm already hearing all these stories and I am like, let's get it started. And I'm tired of seeing these people come in and then go home and seeing return faces on top of people crying about "Oh they gave me three months." By the time I got my time, I was still on my downward spiral because, after I got my time, the sentencing, it was like, that was the rest of my life. Eight years at nineteen years old so I'm not a model prisoner at the time, but I think that is when some of the stuff started to settle in.

When you're in jail you just preparing for prison. How you're supposed to act, what you're supposed to do. At that time, I am learning how I needed to be. But prison is completely different from jail. Jail is like camp. We got a bunch of kids in there, we ran things, eighteen and nineteen year old's. There was a bunch of us. We controlled the dormitory cause we outnumbered everybody else, and we did what we wanted to. Not fighting, not bullying really. We just did what we wanted to. So, by the time I get my time I'm ready to go. They're not telling me anything. Month after month I am still here and now I am getting rowdy, arguing with correctional officers and stuff, down there fighting in the dormitory taking peoples trays and food, being a bully there in the city jail. I'm young and I'm big and I don't care.

Eventually they get me out of there and I get shipped to Deep Meadows. Deep Meadows is where I learned to kind of calm down. I met some guys that I was cool with. They were like "You're young and you got eight years, but it is not the rest of your life. You're gonna turn that eight years into 88 years the way you're acting. You're fighting, you stab somebody, you catch another body, anything." At the time I was just reacting.

Somebody does this, react, I'm not a punk, react, react. When I went to prison, I never stepped into prison like I am the biggest, baddest thing in there. I'm not talking trash, I'm still staying to myself, but my reaction to any slight you do to me is gonna draw a reaction, that was my mindset at the beginning. And you don't know who to trust. "You need anything, man? I'm from Lynchburg!" Just because you're from the same town doesn't mean anything, "Yo, Lynchburg, we got you man. You need anything just come to me".

I got a lot of information, so I was prepared. Even though you're prepared you're still not prepared. I knew what to expect, I knew how it was going to be, I knew the dormitories would have guys from all over Virginia. I knew what to do and what not to do. I wasn't going to go in like I owned the place, all boisterous and loud. Guys told me, "When you go in there, come in with your eyes open. You ain't got to say a lot," but I'm already like that anyway, so I just surveyed, saw what was going on. They said be leery when people come up to you and offer you this or that, you know 'I'm good'. And luckily I didn't need a lot. I had my family that would send me money and there was always Meredith. Meredith would send me money once a month, every other month. And that was enough to help me get the things I needed or I wanted. I didn't have to rely on a lot of people to let me borrow this or that. And we'd get these little jobs in jail, and they'd pay you a little money, not a lot, about thirty dollars a month, but it was something to help you by, whatever you needed.

***

Darrin put me on his visitation list so I could come see

him. This meant driving for several hours to the prison and then going through visitation processes. Sometimes the wait was ridiculously long and the COs never seemed to be in a hurry. I'd show my ID, fill out some paperwork and wait. Once I was called, I entered a small room with a female CO and she would pat me down thoroughly. They had a list of appropriate clothing visitors could wear and ones you couldn't. I was always dressed conservatively and generally had no problems in this area. Young women who were hoping to see their boyfriends sometimes dressed provocatively and were sent home, much to their dismay.

Once I was checked in, I had to wait until I could see Darrin. They didn't want me to arrive at the visitation room too early, so I would often sit there by myself wondering where Darrin was, because sometimes they'd have to find him. He could be sitting in his cell, eating in the cafeteria, or out in the yard for exercise. It always seemed so stupidly inefficient to me. I would've been happy to let someone at the prison know exactly when I would be visiting so Darrin could be ready. Instead, they'd do a "Where's Waldo?" search for him, and I have to believe they'd get distracted at times or simply lose interest in finding him expediently. Any way you put it, prison is a waiting game.

The visitation room in Deep Meadows was funky with an institutional smell that was stale and downright unpleasant, but this was true of every prison that I went to subsequently. A guard would tell me where to sit in the rows of small tables and chairs. Family members, girlfriends or just friends were visiting other inmates, so when I arrived, many of the chairs were already filled. At one end of the room were the vending machines. Inmates weren't allowed to use them since they can't handle money, but visitors can bring some change in a clear baggie and purchase candy, crackers, soda and other items. On my first visit I couldn't buy Darrin anything because I didn't know the rules, but from then on I made sure to hit my change jars at home before I left.

While I waited in the visitation room that first time, I tried not to stare at anyone, but I was intrigued with my surroundings. Finally, Darrin arrived from somewhere in the prison and joined me. I was so happy to see him. He seemed a little thinner, but not much. We hugged each other briefly and sat down to spend the time we were allowed. Just like any other time in our lives, we never had a problem figuring out what to say to each other. Of course we talked some about his situation and how he came to be locked up, but that was the past now. I was more interested in how he was doing now. I was curious to know why he'd made the choices he did. He didn't say a lot. I still felt he was somewhat lost after his mother passed and he did not handle unsupervised adulthood well.

"So, how are you?" I asked.

"I'm good," Darrin responded.

"Have you adjusted to this place?"

"I'm getting in to a routine. I did the crime and I have prepared myself to do the time. I don't have anyone to blame but myself."

"Yes, I guess there are no do-overs at this point," I said

with a smile. I wanted him to know that I supported him in this new situation, but I also felt like I should reiterate the importance of making good decisions. "I've always told you how important it is to make good decisions. That never changes. You need to do the same while you are locked up."

He was still very young. There wasn't a good reason for me to push him. After all, the past could not be changed. I felt my role was to help him come to terms with what he did, to understand that it was wrong, and of course, decide what he was going to do during the years ahead where he will be incarcerated. No matter where you are, you still have to make good choices in life. Darrin took full responsibility for what he had done and the consequences that followed. I was glad about that. Having a level head and being grounded in reality was crucial for Darrin's survival while incarcerated.

"What's the situation with the vending machines? I see people going over to them, but I could not bring any money in."

"You can. You have to bring change and it has to be in a clear baggie. I can't buy anything from the vending machines, but you can," he said.

"Damn. I didn't know. Next time I visit we will get you some good junk food," I said with a smile. "Have you met anyone you can be friends with?"

"I've met a few guys, but I stay to myself a lot right now. I'm not anxious to get into anything I can't handle so I'm mostly watching and learning what I need to do."

"That sounds good. Sounds like a good choice."

A lot of times I am quiet. I guess I'm an introvert. Listening is my nature, watching and listening and picking things up. Until I get comfortable enough around people to mingle. I can mingle with anybody but that's not my normal. I'm only loud when I trash talk, only when someone is thick with me enough to where I can talk a little trash, be obnoxious. But I've always been like that. It's funny cause I've got friends and associates who have never seen me like that and then they'll see me around Curt and we go at each other and talk some smack and they say you always seem so quiet. But some moods I'm more quiet and listening and some moods I am more talkative and joking and laughing. It's definitely about being comfortable with someone. Especially going into new places, or in a room full of people. I look at how they interact or how others I trust might interact with them. It's just who I am. Prison might have had something to do with that. A smart person would judge what's going on instead of just coming there and jumping in.

***

Darrin called me collect every weekend and we would talk about things going on in his life and things going on in my life. I would visit him at least once a month, sometimes more often, and we'd write to each other regularly. Mail is especially important when in prison, and I tried to keep my own letters upbeat and chatty. His letters were well written, and on paper he expressed emotions that allowed me to get a read on his well-being.

He had been dating a Lynchburg girl, Kim, before his arrest and she was hanging in there and visiting him often. I didn't really know Kim, and I didn't have any confidence that the relationship would last, but it did for quite a while and she visited him regularly, often bringing his sister, and her best friend, Bernice. It's a curious thing, but a lot of females attach themselves to men behind bars. Maybe there's some comfort in knowing they have to be faithful, or it's because inmates are more focused on their woman, giving emotional support and attention in the limited way they can. I don't know. I know Darrin's mom truly loved Fred without ever spending time with him outside prison walls. Their marriage was real to her and real to him, and Patricia had hope for their future, so maybe that is all that matters.

Inmates are often moved between different prisons while they serve their time. Darrin was usually moved to prisons close enough that I could see him and return home the same day. Prisons are ranked by security levels and inmates are assigned accordingly, based on their crimes and how well they are doing their time. The highest, a Level 5 prison like Wallen's Ridge State Prison and Red Onion State Prison, are known as SuperMax prisons well known for their strict rules and 23-hour lockdown living conditions for prisoners. Darrin had an old friend who was in Level 5.

When Darrin was around 11 or 12, he would sometimes bring his friend, Little Mike, along with us to get pizza. Little Mike had a slight build and couldn't have weighed any more than 95 pounds. He was a light-skinned fellow who was typically quiet and polite. It was easy for me to forget he was in the back seat of the car when we were heading out for some grub. When Little Mike was 17 or

18, I heard he was arrested for robbing local convenience stores and was sentenced to over 60 years at Red Onion. Whatever he did must have been really bad to have his entire life stripped away and sent to a dismal prison on an isolated mountain in the western wilds of Virginia. I have never been able to make the connection in my mind between the boy who was Darrin's quiet friend and the young man who became a felon. I have to wonder how in the world Little Mike has survived.

Fortunately, Darrin was primarily sent to low-level prisons during the time he served out his sentence. After Deep Meadows, he went to Coffeewood Correctional Center (Level 2), Buckingham Correctional Center (Levels 3 & 4), James River Correctional Center (Level 1) and Powhatan Correctional Center (Mixed Levels). All of these prisons were within a reasonable distance of where Joe and I were living. I usually made the trip to see Darrin alone. Joe would have gladly gone with me but we both figured short visits would be much better kept between Darrin and me. We had a long history together and would probably get more value from the visits if we focused on one another, rather than bringing in someone new for him to build trust with. The only time Joe had ever even seen Darrin was when he was shackled and being led to the department of corrections vehicle. Joe knew how much Darrin meant to me, and he understood that the day would come where he would have the opportunity to get to know Darrin and embrace him fully, too. He looked forward to that day.

***

I got my GED while I was in there. I knew I needed it. A guy told me "You've got to learn something. You've got to work your mind as well as work your body, it's not just about working out. Get a trade, go back to school, or whatever".

So, the first place I went to was Deep Meadows. They had a little GED program. So, I signed up for it, still fresh out of school. When I took my placement test and they saw my scores were high so I didn't really have to go and take classes or anything. They said, "We're going to sign you up for the GED program and you can take the test." I took it there, got my GED there. Then I left, I went to Coffeewood, then Buckingham and it was where I was exposed to the electrical trade. Meredith had been saying the same thing about learning a trade. Buckingham offered electrical and culinary and most guys were going to culinary just so they could eat. But I said nah, I'm not cooking, let's see what electrical is about. Let's do a little electrical course. And I got that under my belt. I left Buckingham to go to James River, and that's where Will was at.

Growing up, I was too young for Will. He would not let me hang around him and his friends and what they were doing. And that's all I wanted. When he first got locked up, he was 18, and I was 14. But he had friends and people I wanted to hang with and chill and he was like no, he always pushed me toward home. He wouldn't let me get involved. He would let me hang around to a certain extent but not for long and he would always kick my butt back home. I knew he was selling drugs or whatever but he wouldn't let me around it or around him when he did it. I understood that part. Will got locked up when he was 18 and then he got back out and went back to prison again. So, we never really spent any time together as adults. The first time we spent time together outside of prison I was in my twenties and he was in his thirties and we were in Norfolk then. I regret now I didn't get to spend more time with Will. I try to do more with him now.

I also understand that Will's childhood was different than mine. He was the oldest, he went through everything first. He had the most responsibility, he babysat us. He understood what it felt like to be poor and not have the money and all that. I don't want to say he was always materialistic. He wasn't, but material things meant something to him. He wanted things and couldn't get them. He saw our mom working two or three jobs and still wasn't getting anything. He had friends who were making money, making more money than my mom, so he just got into it. He liked having stuff.

I know we were brought up the same but his experiences were a little different than mine. I had the buffer of having him, and being able to go to him for things, questions that mom can't answer, life events. He went through it first, dealt with it or dealt with other people, then filtered it for me and braced me for it, help ed me through it. I understand that now. When mom saw him in prison she would bring us with him. We'd go see him as a family. Later, he and I were actually in James River Correctional Facility together for only six months, but it was the happiest six months of my life. You know in prison you're not supposed to be happy, but just being with somebody in prison you know and can trust and not worry about it, that person means the world. You don't know who has ulterior motives and this and that.

When Will was there, I was calm. We did everything together. We ate together, worked out together, everything. We were working on being cellmates, we could have been. He was there before me and he was in like a little honor dorm where they could do special stuff. He had his own bed and his own little space and I was in a dormitory I used to go hang out in his cell while he was at school or work, sit on his bed and eatin' his snacks and stuff.

Chapter 7
A New Reality

We were sorry Darrin couldn't attend our wedding on June 6, 1998. It was an awesome day and we held a very simple wedding in a little white church on Main Street in Wachapreague, where we had first met. My family and Joe's attended, plus our friends from Alabama, Tom and Lynne. Our friend Gaither, who had been there from our first meeting, was also there in the church to help us celebrate. I don't think we could have put together a wedding any better suited for us. Joe and I spent that night in a bed & breakfast in Onancock, but we had to hold off on a real honeymoon so Joe could return to the Navy and I could resume my duties at the newspaper.

Joe finished his 20 years in the Navy and retired three years after we were married, in 2001. He went to work immediately for a really terrific, small, woman-owned company called Intelligent Decision Systems, Inc. (IDSI) based in northern Virginia. This company uses technologists, scientists, and software developers to perform research and analysis, explore data science solutions, apply performance analytics, develop web and software applications, and produce all forms of training and simulation products that ultimately improve performance. Joe's former career made him a natural fit for this work environment. He worked from home, in the office, and oftentimes out of town. He loved what he did, and he was good at it.

As the years passed, keeping close to Darrin remained important to me. I worried about what he was experiencing on the inside, things I couldn't even imagine. There were a few things in Darrin's favor, I reassured my anxious mind, that helped him acclimate successfully to his prison life. He was a big guy, 6'3" and 225 pounds, and a lot less likely to get punked than a smaller man. Darrin was also easy going and smart enough not to act out unless he could be sure of the outcome. Eight years sounds like a lot of time, but in prison, 25 years, 50 years, or life sentences puts his time in perspective. Darrin, unlike many other inmates, had the support of family and friends, and he not only could see that reality, he could feel it. Plenty of guys were locked up who never had visitors or any contact with the outside world at all.

After Darrin had been moved to Buckingham Correctional Center, I made the drive to see him there for the first time. After a typical wait, I was ushered in to the pat down area, where for the first time ever I was asked to take off my bra to make sure I wasn't concealing a weapon or contraband. Maybe it was the underwire that triggered that request. When I was younger I'd gotten in the habit of wearing underwire bras to maximize my small-ish breasts. I'm not sure the slight boost was worth the discomfort, but that's what I happened to be wearing that day. I made a mental note not to repeat that choice on the next visitor's day. On to the next step of processing.

"Those shorts don't meet the length requirements," the screener stated gruffly.

"What?" I replied, shocked. I was in my forties and certainly not trying to impress anyone, especially any of the inmates inside, but when you're as tall as I am, most shorts end up covering less leg than is typical. I'm 5'10." I never dressed provocatively; it wasn't my style.

"Next time you come, remember the guidelines state that shorts and skirts must be below the knee or visitors will be refused entry," she recited in a bored tone.

I knew getting mad wouldn't help me see Darrin that day, so I went out to my car, determined to find a Walmart nearby. Before I left the parking lot, I realized I was wearing a shirt that hung down all over and was pretty long. I could easily pull the waist of my shorts down to rest on my hips and meet their standards. It worked like a charm. Once inside, I breezed through the rest of the screening process and soon found myself at a table in the visitation area.

I couldn't help but notice a young couple across from me as I waited for Darrin to appear. They were flirtatious with one another, as much as they could be under the CO's watchful gaze. Kissing or touching was strictly forbidden, and a brief hug is all that was allowed at the beginning and end of a visit. When the woman got up and walked toward the vending machines, the inmate looked over at me and smiled. I was automatically starting to smile back when I noticed him gather his orange jumpsuit at his groin, proudly revealing the outline of his erect penis. I turned my head and said nothing, shutting out the unwanted sight. "What is wrong with people?" I thought, fighting not to be triggered by the visual assault. Thanks to years of therapy and proper medication, I had learned some good coping tools to preserve my peace when those years of abuse I had endured came to mind. Within minutes, Darrin came out to visit with me. I went to the vending machine to get him some junk food and returned to our table, keeping my eyes carefully guarded, saying nothing to Darrin about the encounter. I was afraid he would confront the guy and punch his lights out.

This was the beginning of our friendship in a very new way. Darrin called me every weekend, and we'd talk on the phone for as long as we wanted. He'd tell me stories from the inside, but only the ones rated "PG," careful to shield me from any horror stories. As I expected he would, Darrin made friends easily no matter which prison he was in. He carried himself in such a way that other inmates respected him and befriended him. Sometimes when I would visit, another inmate would stop by our table briefly to speak to Darrin. I realized I received an edited, watered-down version of his life behind bars, but I began to worry less and less about Darrin as time went on.

***

I didn't' share everything with them when they visited. You don't want anyone to worry. Prison was tough. I learned a lot. I grew up fast. You gotta keep an edge but try not to go too far. You gotta walk a fine line if you want to come home. You gotta pray that nothing happens that jeopardizes that. There's guys that just want to mess somebody's time up. But I've always said, it made me a man. I think I picked up some good things from it. I'm mindful of people's body language, picking up on if there is a lot of tension, survey the area, certain things that, to this day, I still do. Like where I'm sitting in a room. I've got to be facing the door. That's from being in prison.

Joe arranged for Darrin to receive a couple of magazines to help him pass the time, and we also sent money for the commissary so he could order a five-inch screen TV, the largest he was allowed to have in his cell. As he matured, Darrin started filling out and gaining a lot of muscle. While he wasn't always able to use the weights that some prisons provided, he could work out in his cell. There were so many idle hours in the cell that he and some of the other inmates started doing a ridiculous number of push-ups, sit-ups, and whatever else they could do in such cramped quarters. His body and his mind transformed from the scared teenager being led away in handcuffs to a man. While prison isn't the most ideal place to mature and grow, it isn't the worst either. Having your freedom removed creates an environment where you have to think through what you say and do on a daily, even moment-to-moment, basis. Anything less could easily bring about consequences, some of which could be quite severe.

Our prison pic.

When I realized I was good, I guess, at football, I was just naturally good, so it still wasn't discipline and applying myself or working out, cause I'm good, I can step on the field and start doing my thing. Meredith kept telling me you have to work hard, you have to practice and you have to focus. I did it some but I still didn't apply myself as fully as I should because things came easy to me in school and football practice. I didn't have to work, work, work to be the best I could be. I didn't realize until I was older, really until I was in prison and started working out, getting in shape and thinking "I'm in better shape now than I have ever been, even in high school." I realized I had never really focused and thought about what if I had focused.

***

Occasionally, the prisons would have a photo day and I could get my picture taken with Darrin. In one we took together at Buckingham, Darrin wore a light blue jumpsuit and I was in my street clothes. I always find that a hard photo to look at, such stark evidence of Darrin's unfortunate circumstance. It always made me feel good when he and I talked about his crime. He never tried to blame it on anything or anybody else. He knew what he had done was wrong, and he intended to serve out his sentence in the best way he could. He was never a whiner as a kid, and I was glad he wasn't a whiner during his incarceration.

Darrin's girlfriend, Kim, was a bright spot in his life. She often drove from Lynchburg to visit him and they wrote letters to one another. They talked about marriage and even started planning a wedding before they decided to slow things down. I was happy with that decision because I knew that wouldn't be the right move for Darrin at this point in his life. I knew Kim wanted to be true to Darrin while he was behind bars, but eight years is a long time for someone that young and attractive. Darrin had little to give to Kim while he was locked up. Despite their decision, Darrin was still hopeful for a future with Kim and he continued to look forward to her visits. During one occasion, he and Kim were talking at an outdoor picnic table at Buckingham and another inmate started making sexual comments to Kim. Darrin told him to stop and when he didn't, Darrin hit him and a fight ensued. Years later, Darrin explained that whole prison respect thing to me and I got it, but wondered if it had been worth the penalty he paid.

***

When I got in trouble and got shipped out, that was one of the saddest days of my life. Will was upset that I got in trouble. Well, not upset at me cause he understood, but upset that it happened, that they were going to ship me off. In theory I guess I could have not done anything but it wouldn't have went well. I would have had more trouble down the road. That's definitely what I don't need with, like, 18 months left. I mean, I could have 18 months and they might do something to me and Will might not want me to get involved but then he does something. If I hadn't done something, everyone would know that and then the next time she visited me he might be even more aggressive. Especially if she didn't do anything or didn't tell me, so if he thinks its ok and he's going to do this or this or this. You gotta nip stuff like that in the bud.

***

Not long after the incident, Darrin was transferred to Wallens Ridge State Prison. It was located on top of a mountain at Big Stone Gap, near the western border of Virginia. It was cold and isolated and the distance from where Joe and I lived in Chesapeake made a visit impossible to do in one day. There were over 1,000 inmates housed in Wallens Ridge and it allowed a lot less freedom than Darrin had experienced thus far. This was a 23-hour lockdown facility and I was not happy about this change. He could have avoided this if he had made a better decision, which meant him not getting in a fight with that guy over a girlfriend. As it turned out, all of what Darrin went through was pretty much for nothing. Kim got involved with a man on the outside, got pregnant, and ended her relationship with Darrin not long after he was transferred, though they are still close friends and she is close with Darrin's sister, Bernice.

I only went to see Darrin once at Wallens Ridge State Prison, the worst place on earth as far as I was concerned. It was winter, and the road to the prison was icy from the cold and snow, the vegetation alongside heavy and sagging with the weight of accumulated fresh white powder. The farther I drove up the mountain, the more snow there was. When I reached the top, the bleak penitentiary, completely ringed by razor wire, loomed before me like death dug out of a mountainside. Wallens Ridge was no joke. This was a place where pellet guns and stun guns were used to keep order. Racial tensions were an ongoing reality. I wanted to cry thinking about Darrin inside those walls.

Visitation there was similar to the other prisons, except once you were cleared for the visit you had to talk to the inmate through a glass partition, just like you see on television shows and movies. On opposite sides of the cold glass, I don't remember what we talked about, but was just glad to see him and know that he was physically healthy. I couldn't tell much about Darrin's emotional state; if he was distressed, he hid it from me well. I couldn't believe that he had wound up in this dire situation for the crime that he committed. He had been a good kid with no previous record who had dealt unwisely with the personal tragedy of losing his mother. I accepted that he had to be punished under the law, but I just could not understand why Darrin had to be subjected to this extreme sort of consequence after he got into a scuffle with the inmate at Buckingham.

***

When I sit back and think, it kinda flew by. It was a long time but it went by fast. I think I was at Buckingham the longest, I was there for a couple of years. Meredith came and saw me at all of them. I think the hardest one might have been Wallen's Ridge cause we were right on the tip of Virginia in the mountains, that was crazy. When Kim came, most of the time she brought Bernice with her. Even when Kim left for a little while, Bernice still made it up there. Bernice and Kim and Meredith were the most consistent.

Darrin in front of his childhood home on Gilmore Circle.

Chapter 8
Sweet Release

Darrin did not have to stay at Wallens Ridge that long, for which we were both very thankful. The penitentiary system planned to release him after he served seven years and some change. Darrin still had a couple of months to serve, and it was a difficult time for him. Wallens Ridge was home for violent inmates serving life or other lengthy sentences. Oftentimes, if a lifer learns that another inmate is due for release, he might deliberately try to mess it up. With nothing to lose, picking a fight or planting contraband on the short-timer could be easily done. Darrin was aware of this disgusting behavior and stayed to himself for those last weeks. I talked to him often during this last stretch and he assured me there was nothing anyone could do to make him mess up. He was getting out.

In 1995, Darrin had finally served his time and was released from prison. His sister, Bernice, and his Uncle, Steve, made the trip to western Virginia to greet Darrin when he walked out of that place to freedom and took him home to Lynchburg. At the very bottom of the mountain as you leave Wallens Ridge there's a Long John Silver's which was their first stop. I wish I could have been with them to see Darrin inhale fast food, a wonderful contrast to the institutional food he had consumed for so long. I didn't go to Darrin's release as I thought I should be respectful of his family at a time like that. Willie, Darrin's older brother, was locked up when he was in his late teens for selling low level drugs. He had served his time and was released, but eventually gravitated toward selling again and ended up serving more time. Bernice was doing well. I had always considered her be a tough one, and a smart one. No matter what happened to her, she found a way through it and ended up on top.

***

Bernice and Uncle Steve picked me up. That might have been the happiest time of my life, if not it's a close second to the time I spent with Will. One thing I did in prison was try not to get my hopes up high. Because certain things happen, like, I think it might have been an issue when Meredith came to visit me and there was an issue with her shorts and she couldn't get in. Visits could be denied for stupid stuff so if you get your hopes up thinking somebody's going to come and then they're not going to come. People are always saying this thing is going to happen on this day. I'm never thinking it is going to happen. Even though my release date was coming up, and this was then and it's still sorta true now, I didn't build myself up too much because you don't want a letdown. I don't get too excited about a thing until it happens, that's all. But anyway, my point was, my release date was a certain date and I'm thinking, "I ain't never gonna get off this damn hill." When the day finally came, I'm still, like eh, alright, but they finally called my name. I come out and I'm like ,"Okay." I finally get in there and they give me my stuff, my box of stuff. And they don't give you anything. You get your little state khaki pants and khaki clothes. Your family brings you clothes to change into. Bernice brought me a shirt and jeans and shoes to change into. They got a little place by the gate where you change, which was good. I wasn't going back inside for anything! "We want you to step back in for something" Nope! "You forgot to sign…" Nope! You're gonna have to shoot me, I ain't going back!"

But I didn't get happy until that gate opened. When that gate opened and I walked out and saw Bernice and Steve standing there, that was when everything hit me. Just the ride home, my eyes wide open, looking out the window and talking, it was like missed out on the world. I think the first thing we did was stop at Long John Silver for lunch. Cause it was like a six hour drive. But by the time I got home that Long John Silver tore my stomach up. I wasn't used to all that grease and stuff. Whoo! But like I said, I can never forget Bernice and Steve smiling when I walked out. It was emotional, I think I cried.

***

Before his release I had talked to Darrin a few times to find out what his plans were and offer him options. He could go to Lynchburg and live on his own, or he could come live with Joe and me. There were some obvious practical advantages to living with us, but it would require

Darrin to leave his home and friends behind. I didn't want to push Darrin, but I walked him through the long-term advantages that living with us in Hampton Roads would offer. Job opportunities in our area were more plentiful than in Lynchburg, and we would cover him financially until he got a good start. With us, he'd be in a good environment, with adults who loved him and had the resources to look after him. Joe was the real hero in all of this. He really didn't know Darrin except for what I had told him over the years, but he was willing to step up and offer a helping hand. In fact, he was as hopeful as I was that Darrin would decide to come live with us. To me, it seemed like a no-brainer, but I did understand the lure of being on familiar turf with longtime friends. Darrin now had the freedom to make choices for himself and live his own life.

The initial plan was for Darrin to return to his roots and just unwind with his family and friends. I made it a point not to get in touch with him during this time because I wanted him to figure things out on his own. That way, he would be more invested in whatever first step he would take.

Joe and I had just moved to Chesapeake from our home in Suffolk, which we moved into after we got married. We rented a small, but nice, condo in Chesapeake until we found a house to buy. If Darrin came to live with us, he would get the spare bedroom on the second floor. I was stressed about that because the room was so small that it was probably no bigger than the prison cells he had lived in for so many years. If he decided to live with us, at least the door to his room would always open so he wouldn't be stuck there.

***

I got back to Lynchburg and there were friends and acquaintances there to celebrate with me. But before I even came home, you have to have a home plan before they release you. If not, it just seems like a halfway house.

Before I came home, I had to let them know what my plan was and what I was going to do. So, me and Meredith had discussed me living with her instead of settling in Lynchburg. It wasn't like she had to do a lot of convincing. It was the best option. There wasn't a lot Lynchburg had to offer other than familiar faces, family, and friends. But as far as moving on and starting a new life, my odds were better with coming to the Tidewater area, which was bigger, and finding a career. I always knew that was a better option. Even though I knew that, it was still hard because you come home, you've been gone so long, and everything you know, everyone you know is there. That familiarity starts seeping in, everything is there. Going away from that, it was so hard, so emotional. I spent a week in Lynchburg then I moved down [to live with Meredith and Joe].

Meredith was ready to come and get me earlier than that because I had a coming home party Bernice put on and a friend of mine, Calli, was there that night. We were always good friends. I wish we would have been more. She was always a good girl. And I was close to her mom too, Mrs. Bruce. Her mom was worried. She had stopped by, and she saw people smoking weed outside. Now that was outside and I was inside. I wasn't smoking anything and what people did outside was their business. So, when she saw all this, I guess she felt that I could get in trouble again after just coming home, and she called Meredith and told her, "He's running around with some bad people and they're smoking and he might get in trouble." So, Meredith called me up and she was like "Look, I'm coming up there, I'm on my way". It was like the middle of the night and she was coming to get me that night. I'm like "What? Wait. What are you talking about?" She said "I got a call from Mrs. Bruce saying you're around some people and you might get in trouble. I am coming to get you right now."

It was the first or second day I was home, and so I'm like, "No, no, no. Meredith, I understand you're worried." At this time, I already know I am not going to let anybody else jeopardize my freedom, and I conveyed that to her. I knew she was worried. She was ready to come up in the middle of the night, on top of a three and a half hour drive, so I said, "No Meredith. I'm good, I'm fine."

Chapter 9
Homecoming II

I was relieved when Darrin told me his decision. He wanted to live with me and Joe. I was elated, and Joe was looking forward to getting to know Darrin. The plan was to meet in Crewe, Virginia, about halfway between Chesapeake and Lynchburg, at a large convenience store on the outskirts of town. I went alone as Joe had to work, getting there early to make sure I didn't miss him. It was a sunny day, and I was excited for Darrin to be out on his own and starting a new life. I got out of my car, leaned on the hood and just breathed. I know it wasn't me who was locked up for almost eight years, but I had felt locked up inside for Darrin the entire time. The worry, anxiety and distance were gone now, and I felt blessed, so thankful he was coming to live with us.

A car pulled in the parking lot, and I could see Darrin in the passenger seat and that the driver was Darnell! It had been years since I had seen him, and the three of us had a big ol' hugfest right there in the parking lot. It was so good to see my fellas, and now they were men. Darnell had a bushy head of hair that I teased him about and Darrin could be mistaken for a 25 year-old man on steroids.

We visited for a while and then headed out, Darnell to Lynchburg and Darrin with me to Chesapeake. We had a relaxed conversation and enjoyed the ride. I could tell how relieved Darrin was to be free, but like any young person starting out, I could also sense he was apprehensive about the future. I apologized ahead of time about how small his room was, but he was grateful that he could leave the house anytime he wanted.

Staying with us would give Darrin the opportunity to get to know Joe, and that was important to me because I wanted Darrin to benefit from Joe's influence. In my mind, we were bringing in family, but I knew that in Joe's, we were inviting someone who was almost a stranger to him. Joe was good at putting people at ease, and I knew the time spent with Darrin would soon make their relationship natural, as though they had known one another for a long time.

***

I was always grateful. When Joe and I met, I had known Meredith for years. It didn't mean Joe and I were going to be automatic. But I remember he was real cool and I tell this story to most everybody I meet. When I first moved down to Chesapeake, I was going out and I didn't know anybody and I was stuck at a club called Blakely's one night. I needed a ride at one or two o'clock in the morning and I called Joe and Meredith. I felt bad for waking them up but Joe just came and got me and that meant the world to me.

***

One evening after dinner, Darrin and I threw the football in the narrow alley behind our townhouse. I had not thrown in years, possibly not since he was a boy. My passes were weak, but I was amazed how far he could throw that ball. He had been building muscle, and it translated into some unbelievable distance on his passes. For a moment, I imagined that he'd gone to college instead of prison and played football on a Division I team. Before everything happened, I had taken him to a football game at the University of Virginia and he loved it and became a big fan. No use imagining what could have been, though. Life is what it is.

After we finished throwing the football, we sat out in the garage and talked, sipping on cold beer and reminiscing. Somehow we got on the subject of women, and Darrin admitted he was shy about getting out to have a good time and meeting people his own age. I told him to clean himself up and I would give him enough money to sit at the bar at a nearby Friday's restaurant and see what happened. When I dropped him off at Friday's, I hoped he would have a good time. Darrin has always been a good-looking guy, and maybe just some time on his own in that environment would help him feel better. The Friday's was close enough where he could walk home or catch a cab. I didn't see Darrin again before I went to bed, but the next day he was all smiles. That one evening helped him to find his confidence and he never looked back.

Joe and I had a motorcycle that we'd purchased mainly because I saw it for sale in the classifieds and suddenly decided we needed it. Joe wasn't really on board, but he'd learned not to try to shut me down when I got excited like that. We went to the seller's house, looked it over, and bought it. We took motorcycle riding classes to learn the rules and be able to drive safely. We had been riding for a while when Darrin came to live with us. Darrin was itching to take it out, but he still didn't have a driver's license and hadn't taken the required safety course. I told him if he wanted a ride, he could hop on with me. He got on the back and I headed to the Interstate where we could go fast. Cars passing us on either side were craning their necks to look at us. We must have been quite a sight, a slender 45-year-old white lady driving, with a 25-year-old black dude wearing a wife beater covering huge muscles adorned with prison tattoos, hanging on behind me. I smiled as we zipped down the Interstate. This was just us, and we didn't have a care in the world.

During the time of the "famous motorcycle ride." Darrin had not been with us for long and he was really buff from his time incarcerated. Fortunately, he came out wiser and stronger.

After some time, Joe and I asked Darrin about his requirements as a newly released offender. He had it down. He'd been assigned to a parole officer and had to meet her on a regular basis, so I gave Darrin a ride to his first meeting. His parole officer was a young woman of about 24 or 25. She met with Darrin privately and instructed him in what he needed to do, and what he'd better not do. Showing up for meetings with her as scheduled, on time, was one of the biggest things he had to remember. I wish the other things he had to tackle were as easy as that requirement, but they were not.

I can see why so many incarcerated people return to prison after a few months outside because the system seems to be set up to make released felons fail. Their first priority is to pay off the court costs incurred at the time of their arrest. For most, to do that means you must be able to earn money, so getting a job is critical. However, even if you're fortunate enough to be employed, you can't get a driver's license until court costs are paid, which makes it pretty damn tough to get to your job. This is a vicious circle that no one could manage on their own with the few available resources most inmates have upon release.

One of the first things Joe and I did was pay off Darrin's court costs with the understanding that he'd repay us once he got his feet on the ground. To adhere to the ridiculous rules about how this should be handled, in the easiest way, I asked my parents, who still lived in Lynchburg, to go down to the courthouse and pay Darrin's court costs in cash. In the meantime, we mailed them a check to replenish their bank funds. With that behind us, Darrin could get his driver's license, so we started looking for an inexpensive used vehicle for him. Darrin really liked an older model Jeep that was in good shape, so we bought it, tacking the amount on to what he already owed us. Joe and I knew we would go easy on what he owed us because we tend to be softies. We didn't want Darrin to know that, though, because he needed to take his responsibilities seriously, make payments and learn to take care of himself in the real world.

With his court costs paid and a license to drive his vehicle, Darrin started looking for a job. At first he worked as a bouncer at Blakely's, but soon realized he couldn't make much money doing it. It was tough going because almost all of the applications asked if he'd ever committed a felony. I advised him that it's always best to be honest and up front about his past. We told him to be patient and the right opportunity would come along. Thankfully, that is exactly what happened. He was hired by a company who was wiring homes and condominiums and needed a helper. This job didn't require any special skills, but Darrin liked the work environment and the people he worked with. He basically served as a back up to the electricians doing the work, getting tools, hauling away debris, and other manual tasks. As he worked, Darrin paid attention to what they did and decided he really liked this kind of work.

On one of his first jobs, he worked with a guy named Don. He was a good electrician who took the time to teach Darrin things about the trade. Darrin had taken courses in electrical work during his incarceration, so he already knew the basics. Don was thoughtful and a good teacher who was patient, but kind of a loner. Darrin got to know him pretty well over the time they worked together and really liked him. Bob was thorough when he showed Darrin how to do some of the work and I think he may have been a catalyst for Darrin moving forward in this field.

***

When I first came home I wanted to get into electrical. I was looking for jobs and I got one as an electrician's helper. When I first met Don I did not think he was the one who was going to teach me a lot. When you looked at Don, he was quiet. He doesn't talk a lot. He kept to himself. He never talked about girls or anything. I don't know if he had a girlfriend. He talked about being able to go home and play his PlayStation and be comfortable at home. He was really, really antisocial. But after a while he started showing me things and explaining stuff to me. Of course, he had to cause at that time I didn't know anything.

An example of that was, we were working and we had scraps of copper from pulling Romex through these houses and cutting scraps off when you're tying everything up and you got a big box with copper in it, and I am thinking it is like a trash box. I didn't know at the time that you could get money for copper, so the box was to be taken to the shop at the end of the job. Some guy comes by and yells, "Hey man!" and I'm working and Don is somewhere else, "Hey man! What you gonna do with that box of copper out there?" I'm like, "That's trash man. You can have it," not thinking of what he wants it for. Later that day or the next day, Don says, "Hey, have you seen that box of copper?" and I said, "Yeah, some guy came and asked me and I told him it was trash and he could have it." Don was like, "No, no, no, no, no, no!" and he explained right there and then, "That's money, we've got to turn that back into the company". I had no clue. I think it was good that he actually explained that to me 'cause I would have been giving stuff away. He took me under his wing and showed me stuff which was also good for him cause I was his helper. We didn't have a lot of lengthy conversations, but Don was a good guy. He showed me a lot. The time I spent with Don might have been a little less than a year, but I learned a lot of residential stuff that I didn't learn in the union. That little time with him was a good experience. It added a lot to my knowledge.

People don't want to show you or teach you things if you act like you already know everything. If you are always talking, how are you going to learn like that? So, I know it's important to watch and to look. And some people don't like to talk, so it is good to just watch. They might do something and they might not want to tell you, but they want you to watch, "By me doing it in front of you, I am showing you."

By that time ,I had a friend from back home, Dee, who lived in Newport News, and he was in the union. Once we met up and talked he said, "Yo, you gotta join the union." And he told me all about the apprenticeship, and what I could do. So, he was the reason I joined the apprenticeship. I might've stayed with Don and that company and been fine. But they put me in school to actually become an electrician. They had a program. Once I talked to the apprenticeship director, told him I had a *record, and asked if I could go through the program and would I still be able to work. He said,, "Yeah, it's not a problem. We understand that." Once he told me that I was like, "Okay, I am going to join." At that time that was the road to take. I was looking for something.*

***

Joe and I were pleased to see Darrin building on this future. He'd worked long enough to figure out that he would need more schooling to obtain higher paying jobs. Darrin took steps to get his life on the right trajectory by joining the International Brotherhood of Electrical Workers, Local 1340, and signing up for classes, with the goal of becoming a journeyman electrician. The program was taught over a period of several years and the classes didn't interfere with work, so Darrin could keep earning money while readying himself to do more. Darrin had looked at the benefits of getting further training with the union and knew how much money he could make if he completed the course.

I admit that I did not think he would stick with it. The classes required a lot of math and memorization regarding installation of new electrical components and the maintenance and repair of existing electrical infrastructure. It was like being back in high school, only much more demanding, and Darrin had never liked high school. Those years of being locked up changed Darrin more than I thought, because he not only completed the course and became a journeyman electrician, he scored high marks along the way. He went to class faithfully three nights a week for over three years and graduated. We were so proud of Darrin!

Darrin at work.

I just see it as something that you have to do. If you're going to make it work, you have to move forward, and you gotta put in the work. Go to school or go to work or whatever.

I try not to look at things in the negative. I think I am upbeat. I try to look at the bright side of things when something happens, especially if you can't control it and there's nothing you can do about it, why worry about it?

***

Joe and I decided we were ready to move out of the small rental and found just what we wanted around the corner on Crystalwood Circle off Battlefield Boulevard in Chesapeake, Virginia. It was less than two miles from where we lived, so the move was much easier than most. Darrin got a bigger bedroom this time around, but by now we weren't seeing as much of him because he was working, out with friends, or with women that he dated. We moved to Crystalwood Circle in November 2005 and lived there until June, 2007, a period of time in which Darrin came into his own. He was in his mid-twenties, was moving up in his work, making more money, and living a good life. Toward the end of Darrin's time with us, I would be making coffee in the morning when occasionally I'd notice a young woman slip by the kitchen and let herself out. That was the sign that it was time for us to nudge Darrin out of our nest. He was ready, and although he was appreciative of living with us, he was an adult now and wanted to live like one.

***

I'm sure Meredith was still sort of thinking I'm still young, I'm still learning. But by this time I had grown. I'm not saying I was a hardened man, but I had seen things and I had grown and I had also made determinations in my life like, I am not going to prison again. I'm older, my mind is more mature. I don't just weigh things different, I didn't weigh anything before! And I didn't need eight years to realize that, it could have been two or three, I've learned my lesson.

So, I already knew, I am never going back. A lot of what I did was to escape reality, hanging out with friends, smoking weed, or just chilling was just a way of dealing with shit you need to deal with. I've never been like 'boo-hoo' when I got out cause I knew I was lucky to have Joe and Meredith in my corner. I know a lot of guys who don't have that support system or anyone in their corner to push them, or to let them know 'Hey man, you might mess up a little, but get back on track.' But on top of that, you gotta be ready to make a change in your life, cause even with a support system, if you're not ready to change or do right you're not gonna do right anyway.

I knew coming back, I had to take advantage of the opportunities I had. Even when I first came home, I still didn't take full advantage as I should have. I was young, it was my first time being out, first time being in a bar. I needed to get it out of my system. Meredith was talking about 'you gonna save up? I'm discovering people and people are discovering me, women are looking at me for the first time differently than ever in my whole life. I was always a little chunky kid. I come home and I'm in shape and so all this stuff was new to me. It might not have been the most fun but it was the happiest, that first year and a half, after I got past the first awkward stage in the first month or two.

***

I became tired of the newspaper business for a number of reasons. I wanted out. I had worked in several low-level jobs from the very beginning and then started working for the military newspapers division. This was stimulating work at the outset and required travel to military bases across the United States. Most of my work was in Camp Lejeune, North Carolina and Fort Hood, Texas. I was away from Joe a fair amount, but I was home on most weekends and we were able to make it work. Being away so much wasn't ideal, and the same toxic newspaper culture was alive and well in the military division, so I needed to take a break.

I landed a job as a stainless steel and aluminum

salesperson for E.J. Enterprises, located in Glen Burnie, Maryland. They assigned me a territory from Richmond to Norfolk, and in the first year I made significant progress in revenue gains. I really liked the guys who ran the company, E. Johnson and Hal Odum, but it wasn't meant to be a career decision. I returned to the newspaper business for ten months, and in 2006, I launched my own magazine business in Williamsburg, Virginia.

My magazine was designed for locals in Williamsburg, so I named it *Next Door Neighbors*. It was tough starting a new publication, and especially difficult since I was starting it from Chesapeake, almost an hour away from Williamsburg. *Next Door Neighbors* was perfect for a market the size of Williamsburg but would have never gained traction in a market as large as Chesapeake. It took a lot of heavy lifting to get the magazine off the ground, but after thirteen months, I finally broke even on an issue and it began to take off from there. Joe and I realized that we would need to move to Williamsburg for the magazine to prosper. At the same time, the company he worked for won a good contract based out of Fort Eustis and they opened an office in Williamsburg. This was a perfect situation for us. In June 2007, we moved, renting a nice home on Durfey's Mill Road. We lived there until September of 2008, when we purchased our present home on Wellington Circle.

Our move to Williamsburg put more distance between me and Darrin, but it didn't change our relationship. We knew we were both in it for life. These recent changes were significant in how I viewed Darrin. He was a man now, and his independence marked a new chapter in our lives. I had to let him go in some ways so that he could continue to find himself and grow into the man he wanted to be. I was so busy getting my magazine off the ground that I really didn't spend a lot of time worrying about him. There was no reason to anyway. Darrin was living his life, and it was his life.

At one point, Darrin dated Diana, a woman a little older than him. She lived at home when I first met her, but it wasn't long after that that she found a nice apartment in downtown Virginia Beach. She was a crane operator at the Norfolk Naval Shipyard. Diana's controls were at the top of the crane. Her job was to pick up and move heavy containers from one location to another. She sat up on her perch almost all day, picking up heavy containers and gently placing them where they needed to go. Diana was white and her parents didn't approve of Darrin. I knew them a little because they had lived next door when we lived on Crystalwood Circle in Chesapeake. That's how Darrin met Diana. Knowing how her parents felt about people of other races, she never wanted them to know about Darrin, and he was good with that for a time. Eventually, Darrin felt like Diana should let her parents know about their relationship. I don't know exactly when they told them but I don't think they were very receptive. He and Diana continued to see one another regardless and moved in together for a while. They had a nice life in Virginia Beach Town Centre.

***

Diana was nice, a beautiful lady, inside and out. But at the time, I thought about what she was going through. She felt she needed to get away from her mom, and I was the little push that got her out of the house. I think we helped each other out at the time, but she really needed more. I wanted to be with her too, but at the same time, I wasn't ready to be in a relationship with one person at that point.

Will and Darrin. Close brothers.

Eventually, Darrin's relationship with Diana ran its course, and it wasn't long before he had another love interest. Her name was Eva. Eva was Hispanic and spoke her native language much better than English. It always amazed me how Darrin could tell what she was saying in Spanish while I could only pick out random words that I couldn't string together to make sense. I guess when you're motivated and spend a lot of time with someone, you learn to understand.

Darrin had strong feelings for Eva. They were together for about ten years. During that time, they took several trips together including one to Spain where Darrin met Eva's parents. They also found a great deal on a foreclosure and purchased it, moving in together. I had visions of babysitting a little Darrin one day. I had never known Darrin to be this devoted to a woman. But it came to an end, and Darrin seemed at peace with that. We talked about it, and he told me he didn't think he would ever get married. I didn't pry into his feelings or what had happened between them. I just told him that not everyone was meant to be married and it was certainly fine if that wasn't something he wanted for his future. Darrin never had any trouble meeting women. He was a good-looking man, and he was good to women. He had always held his mother in high regard and felt like he got his strength and compassion from her, which carried over into his relationships with women. My hope for him was that he would experience the full depth of a relationship built on trust and commitment. I didn't necessarily think he had to be married to find that, but I did think marriage was important, and it had made all the difference in my life.

Darrin's brother, Will, was released from prison around this same time. He had been in and out for about 16 years.

All of his convictions had been for selling low level drugs. I didn't know Will very well when he first got out, and he can be a bit shy, but Darrin helped him with the transition by sharing his apartment with him. When Darrin and Eva moved in together, Will kept Darrin's studio apartment.

Like Darrin, Will was anxious to embark on a better life. He got some training in HVAC and found employment in that area. He was done with his old way of life. Will had been married years before and had a daughter, but that relationship didn't survive all of his years of incarceration.

Will, Curtis, Darrin and my husband, Joe, on our back porch.

I think that's our family, me, Will, and Bernice are not he most social right off. We are careful approaching a public setting or a crowd. Even though I can get in there I might need a push.

Bernice and I fought like crazy as kids, still do. Sometimes Will is still playing referee. She says something I don't like or I say something she doesn't like and trip, trip, tripping. Kim, her best friend, tells us it's because we are so much alike, that's why we bump heads, you're different in your own way but you're more alike than you like to think. Both of you are stubborn and both of you want things your own way. And that's probably right. We're more alike than I guess me and Will. Will is more flexible. But he is internal too. He's the type of person who will let stuff build up and bother him until it explodes. I'm going to speak my mind. If it affects me, I'm going to speak up.

***

Once Will was released, Joe and I saw a lot more of him. He and Darrin would make many trips to Williamsburg to hang out with the two of us, or we would go to them and take them to dinner. The four of us have had some great times and good laughs over the most most recent years. Sometimes we stay home and the fellas, including Curtis who is also a part of our circle, play Dominoes and thoroughly enjoy ourselves. Darrin, Will and Curtis honed their Dominoes skills in prison, but once Joe learned the game he would always give them a good run. I didn't ever care about playing. It was always fun to watch them. Like Darrin, Will has a great sense of humor, and we laugh, drink, and make fun of each other. Sometimes we go out to places like our local Chowder Fest, usually held in November. It's cold at that time of year, but the tents are heated and we could stay warm as we went from booth to booth to sample the chowders prepared by different area restaurants. Other times we hang out at Paul's Deli in New Town. They have an outdoor fire pit which keeps us cozy while we eat dinner and follow up with cigars.

*The gang: Will, Meredith, Darrin and Curtis
at our home in Williamsburg.*

At the Corner Pocket, another popular spot, we pick teams and shoot pool for hours. Williamsburg Alewerks features a patio like a cubby hole between two buildings and some greenery. During warm days, large umbrellas shade us as more competitive Dominoes ensue. During cooler months, the walled environment makes sitting outside just right and we all love being outdoors.

I turned 60 in 2020, and Darrin will be 43 in 2021. It is hard to believe he was ever my Little, and that our lives, which just yesterday were so far in front of us, are now so far behind. When Darrin was first locked up, I remember telling him I would be 45 when he got out. That was 15 years ago, and Darrin has become the man I always hoped he would be. I am so proud of him. Always. When we talk about meaningful things or text about what is happening in the world that is relevant, we almost always end with, "I love you." There is a short list of those I say "I love you" to, because it is meaningful. You both live your truth, and that truth is respected and protected with those words. No judgement.

*****

I think Meredith and I are closer now because we're both adults and we're more open to communications and comfortable talking to each other and sharing stuff. When I was younger, I may not have been as comfortable about sharing everything. I mean, when I was younger, talking about girls or smoking weed or other personal things, it wasn't something I would talk with Meredith about. It's not what you'd talk with your mom about! I'm not saying Meredith's my mom but she is almost like an aunt to me, almost like a second mom. I've always thought of her like that. Some things I never shared with my mom because of that mother and son dynamic. So, now the friendship, we are both adults, we have been through everything, so the barriers and cautions of not sharing everything aren't there, we're more open. I value her opinion, and Joe's. If I ask them about something it's because I really want to know what they think. I don't do that for a lot of people. I'm going to do my own thing regardless of what anyone else thinks of me or tells me anyway. I also don't let other people's opinions affect me unless they mean something to me. If you mean something to me, like Meredith, Joe, or Nancy; people like that who are close to me, then their opinion actually means a lot to me. But a lot of people don't and I couldn't care less what they think.

Basically, I don't blame anybody for the situation. I might feel that they gave me too much time or they didn't have to do that, but I did what I did and the consequences are the consequences. I can't blame it on the white man or the judge or anything like that. I took it upon myself and I can blame me. I went to prison, I dealt with it, and now I'm out. That's my whole life thing. I try to put stuff behind me. I don't dwell too much in the past or blame. Like my mom's death. Some people say "You probably hadn't fully dealt with it yet," but in my mind I had dealt with it. I put it in a place in my mind, I moved forward. I don't think about it too much. I think I'm in a good place.

It's not like I have a big issue talking about being in prison. For example, me and Will, both of us have been locked up. He finds it hard sometimes to talk about being locked up and stuff like that, I think he doesn't want to tell people because he doesn't want to alienate them or affect their opinion of him. My thing is, it's not like I am proud of it or that it's the first thing I say. But I went there and I learned a lot and it straightened me out. It made me so much stronger than what I was and made me more prepared for life. The trajectory I was on was headed downward and it elevated back up. So, I think maybe I needed that. I needed it to straighten out.

***

As I finish telling our story, we are living in the midst of the harsh realities of COVID 19 and extreme racial unrest from the murders of young black men and women. I think people of all colors want to figure out how to move forward in a better way, but the answer is not simple. So much of what minorities are facing is not under their control. I saw a recent video, Uncomfortable Conversations with a Black Man, (uncomfortableconvos.com) where Emmanuel Acho, who is black, interviewed Matthew McConaughey, who is white. It's a short video, but it touches on what I believe is the core of this matter. What is our responsibility as an individual for making all of our lives better? What will we find when we examine ourselves and what can we do to put our best self out into the world?

When George Floyd was murdered by a white police officer recently, Darrin was truly upset, as was I. He posted this on Facebook: I want to take to the streets and protest so bad but the safest place for me and everyone else is at home. Darrin made the wise decision not to take it to the streets. As a white person, I say that I understand, but I can't be sure that I really do. How could I? I am just happy that Darrin had the wisdom to take the high road. The years that were so difficult for him has taught him to become the kind of man who knows life is all about choices. I think he has made many good choices since the day he left prison.

***

The most racism I dealt with was when I was at Wallen's Ridge. I think I was in there for 16 or 18 months. That was probably the hardest time, just dealing with people, the attitude, mostly from the correctional officers. They hated that Kim was coming up to see me. They would comment on it. "You got this pretty little girl coming up in here. I'm gonna see her" and this and that. I'd just sit there. You can't say too much and I wasn't going to say anything. I was at their mercy. I've seen what they've done to people, like in the hole up there. When I first got there I was in the hole. They didn't treat people good. They abused their power a lot. It wasn't smart to argue with them. So, you take it and you deal with it and you grit your teeth, you know. The power struggle is that they have the power and you don't.

All in all I learned a lot about it, I read a lot. I learned a lot about religion, I learned a lot about government, I've learned a lot about conspiracy theories and stuff like that. Because you've got all types of people there. You've got people who are just angry, looking to blame somebody "the system's fucked up" or whatever. But then you've got certain educated people who have been in there a while who say "Look, check this book out, read this book, tell me what you think. Apply that to yourself and what you've seen and how you've been dealt with or treated." So, you get time to think and a lot of times that's why people jump into religion or become a Muslim or Five Percenter or whatever. One is for protection and the other is because you can look at stuff and think "Okay, the way I came up, the stuff I've been through, how the system treated me, or this or that" you start to see differences. Or start to read up about history or whatever.

I read so much stuff like "The Pale Horseman," "The ISIS papers," books that make you think, stuff I didn't know. But I just thought on a different level than I ever thought before. I allowed myself to think. I think you have to take bits and pieces of information and pull them together and do what's best for you. You can't let anybody make decisions for you.

For example, you can't not like somebody just because someone tells you not to like them. You've got to be around that person, see how that person is, how they treat you, all of that, and then make your own decision. It's a simple example of everything.

***

It's hard to imagine how our lives would have turned out if I had been matched with a different little boy instead of Darrin, and he had been given a different Big Sister. I know my life would have been very different, and I expect his would be, too. I feel so blessed that it went the way it did. We have taught each other how strong love can be, and how pure and powerful it is when there are no hidden agendas. When he was young, I looked after him. Now we look after each other, and we will always have that until one of us dies. Having different skin color and being a different age and gender didn't matter after all. What truly mattered, and still does, is what we put into our relationship. I think we have given each other, and continue to give, our very best selves.

***

I think Meredith influenced my life a lot. If she wasn't in it, I would hate to think how I would be. Because everything I think Meredith did being in my life has been beneficial to me. The things she taught me, her kindness, the little educational lessons. I'm not saying I might not have learned them from anywhere else. I probably would have. But she saw some things when I was younger that probably my mom might have missed. My mom worked all the time. Meredith picked up that I couldn't spell her name, at a young age, and that I had a problem with spelling, so she helped me. Like a big sister. I mean, spelling is still not my strongest suit, but it would have been a lot worse if she hadn't helped me do that part. That's a small example right there, but I learned so much from her. I think that if she wasn't in my life maybe I would have grown to adulthood and been at a disadvantage. Even more of a disadvantage than I was when I came out of prison. She was in my life and I still went to prison, but she has been instrumental in my growth and in my becoming a better person and knowing who I am.

I always felt that if I ever reached out, she would be there. She has always been there for me, throughout my life. Big or small, I can call, and she has always been there.

About the Authors

We only had one reason for writing this book. We felt like we had a great story to tell. So, we decided to tell it. Joe, my husband, helped me by being the sounding board we needed and by interviewing Darrin several times to put his words to paper. Narielle Living and Linda Landreth Phelps, both writers for *Next Door Neighbors*, a magazine I publish in Williamsburg, Virginia, provided guidance, editing expertise and greatly improved our first manuscript.

There are experiences from our lives that Darrin and I recounted that we believe others can relate to, either directly or indirectly. We knew we were putting ourselves out there, but we felt okay about it. We know that no matter what happens in life we can find our way with the help of God, family and friends. The overriding theme, and the subtitle of the book, says it all: *Love has no boundaries.*

CPSIA information can be obtained
at www.ICGtesting.com
Printed in the USA
BVHW021730180422
634619BV00010B/192